SAM CALAGIONE
Dogfish Head Craft Brewery

JASON & TODD ALSTRÖM
BeerAdvocate

PROJECT EXTREME BREWING

AN ENTHUSIAST'S GUIDE TO EXTREME BREWING AT HOME

INCLUDING OVER 50 HOMEBREW RECIPES AND CREATIVE BREWING PHILOSOPHIES FROM DOZENS OF AMERICA'S MOST BELOVED AND COVETED INDIE CRAFT BREWERIES

Inspiring | Educating | Creating | Entertaining

Brimming with creative inspiration, how-to projects, and useful information to enrich your everyday life, Quarto Knows is a favorite destination for those pursuing their interests and passions. Visit our site and dig deeper with our books into your area of interest: Quarto Creates, Quarto Cooks, Quarto Homes, Quarto Lives, Quarto Drives, Quarto Explores, Quarto Gifts, or Quarto Kids.

First Published in 2018 by Quarry Books, an imprint of The Quarto Group, 100 Cummings Center, Suite 265-D, Beverly, MA 01915, USA.
T (978) 282-9590 F (978) 283-2742
QuartoKnows.com

Quarry Books titles are also available at discount for retail, wholesale, promotional, and bulk purchase. For details, contact the Special Sales Manager by email at specialsales@quarto.com or by mail at The Quarto Group, Attn: Special Sales Manager, 401 Second Avenue North, Suite 310, Minneapolis, MN 55401, USA.

ISBN: 978-1-63159-287-4

Digital edition published in 2018

Library of Congress Cataloging-in-Publication Data available

Design: Burge Agency
Photography: Steve Legato, except the following: Hogger & Co. Photography,6; 8; 10; 11; 29; 71; 144; 145; 150; 152; 154; 155; 156 / Kevin Flemming 17; 18; 20; 28; 31; 40 / Shutterstock 19; 23; 24; 27; 30; 31; 36; 38; 39, 41, 42; 48

Printed in China

WE DEDICATE THIS BOOK TO
THE CREATIVE BREWERS WHO
MAKE US THINK AND DRINK
DIFFERENTLY. WITHOUT YOU,
BEER WOULD BE BORING.

Todd and Jason Alström

CONTENTS

PREFACE : BY SAM CALAGIONE

I`M ALWAYS SUPER PROUD WHEN I GET TO THE CUSTOMS BOOTH AT AN AIRPORT SOMEWHERE FAR FROM HOME AND I HAVE TO WRITE DOWN MY OCCUPATION ON THE REQUIRED FORM. I AM PROUD TO WRITE: BREWER. THAT IS MY VOCATION AND MY AVOCATION. I`M A BREWER FIRST AND A BUSINESSMAN SECOND.

The tradition of brewing beer is as old as civilization itself—Literally. The oldest known fermented cereal beverage (the most basic definition of a beer) was brewed around 10,000 years ago in China. That's about the same time in human history when we evolved from being hunting and gathering nomads to settling down into communities to domesticate crops. You might say this was the era when humans evolved socially and stopped competing with each other to hunt down and kill; instead, we started helping each other work the land and raise crops to assure our nutritional sustenance.

The earliest known beer recipe comes from this period in China and includes rice and grapes and hawthorn fruit. I know because Dogfish Head and Dr. Pat McGovern produce a modern interpretation of this early recipe called Chateau Jiahu. When considering this unexpected beer recipe, you might say that the earliest known fermented beverage wasn't just the prototypical beer but the prototypical extreme beer. And it was more than that—as all beers are. It was a catalyst for human interaction, for sustenance, for collaboration, and for creative expression. I have always said the beer community is 99 percent asshole-free. That's true today and I like to think it was true in those early days of fermentation as well.

The recipes in this book can be brewed solo. They could even be consumed solo, if you as the brewer and reader fancy yourself the anti social, loner type. Ideally, they are meant to be shared; to be brewed with friends and family; to be consumed with friends and family; and to serve as catalysts for conversations, interaction, education, and fun. There are really two components of brewing for me that have been existentially rewarding. One: the opportunity to take risks and try ingredient combinations and techniques that may never have been done before. And two: the opportunity to meet, learn from, and be inspired by so many amazing people who have informed my journey as a brewer.

Each and every one of the brewers who have contributed recipes and their philosophies of creative brewing to this book inspire me. To name a few, specifically who are contributors, personal friends, and true evangelist for the brewing community: Charlie Papazian, author of the *Joy of Homebrewing* and founder of the Brewers Association; and Chris Graham of MoreBeer! And, of course, my coauthors of this book Todd and Jason Alström of BeerAdvocate. The craft brewing and homebrewing communities have truly exploded since I wrote my last recipe-oriented book, *Extreme Brewing*, eleven years ago. There are so many more commercial brewers and homebrewers making beers outside the Reinheitsgebot today than there were back then.

I love that this book's pool of contributors has expanded in the same way that our community has since the last book. I truly believe it has been the creativity and infectious joy in sharing beer knowledge in both the homebrewing and commercial craft brewing community that has sparked the explosion of consumer interest in flavor-forward, adventurous beers over the last ten years. We created this excitement ourselves. It was not created by the global brewing conglomerates who spend billions of dollars advertising their light lagers and quasi-craft beers each year.

Each of the fine folks who contributed recipes to this project makes their livelihood in the world of beer, and each of them inspires me by prioritizing passion before profits. I was working on this book intro in a hotel room in New York City recently. I took a break from writing to read Hemingway's *The Sun Also Rises*—a great book about morality and natural beauty, the Lost Generation, and a group of friends drinking numerous glasses of adult beverages together. I got to this passage about bullfighters seen through the eyes of the hotel owner character named Montoya, and it made me think of my beer friends and mentors, all of the brewers who contributed to this book, and all of you readers who are interested in taking some of the recipes within these covers on your own creative brewing journey. It's staccato, repetitious poetry, with a strong sense of purpose as is the best of Hemingway's writing:

"Your friend is he aficionado, too?" Montoya smiled at Bill.

"Yes," I said. "He came all the way from New York to see [the bull-fight]."

"Yes?" Montoya politely disbelieved. "But he's not aficionado like you."

He put his hand on my shoulder again embarrassedly.

"Yes," I said. "He's a real aficionado."

"But he's not aficionado like you are."

Aficion means passion. An aficionado is one who is passionate about the bull-fights. All the good bull-fighters stayed at Montoya's hotel, that is, those with aficion stayed there. The commercial bull-fighters stayed once, perhaps, and then did not come back. The good ones came each year. In Montoya's room were their photographs. The photographs were dedicated to Juanito Montoya or to his sister. The photographs of bull-fighters Montoya had really believed in were framed. Photographs of bull-fighters who had been without afición Montoya kept in a drawer of his desk. They often had the most flattering inscriptions. But they did not mean anything. One day Montoya took them all out and dropped them in the wastebasket. He did not want them around."

I love that passage and its message championing those who never let the tail of commerce wag the dog of inspiration. And I know this craft brewing community and the BeerAdvocate community are building on that foundational spirit. So, my portion of this book is dedicated to the beer evangelists I name above and all of the brewers who contributed their recipes and philosophies within these pages.

Of course, there are many more creative and talented brewers whose recipes didn't make it into this book. We could not fit them all. And the ranks of the great ones—homebrewers and pro brewers alike—are growing. And that is a beautiful thing. But the breadth of contributing brewers represents a broad crosscut of the TRUE AFICIONADOS of our community. Thanks for sharing your thoughts and knowledge with the growing ranks of intrepid and fearless brewers about to embark on their own mission within *Project Extreme Brewing*. Namaste, Y'ALL!

REINHEITSGEBOT

Five hundred years ago, on April 23, 1516, a couple of Bavarian dukes enacted this law. "In all cities and markets and in the countryside," the Reinheitsgebot reads, "only barley, hops, and water may be used for brewing beer." (Yeast was added to the law later, after Louis Pasteur discovered this glorious, single-cell organism was doing the fermenting.)

At the time, brewers sometimes added soot, wood chips, and even toxic roots to beer. So partially, the law was enacted to better regulate brewing ingredients for safety. But experts think the law was really about protecting markets, not consumers. Brewers were barred from using wheat and rye, so that bakers had enough to make bread. The law also capped the price of beer and effectively banned specialty beers from other regions.

I believe the centuries ruled by the Reinheitsgebot have resulted in less diversity and creativity in the global beer marketplace. The regulation may only apply legally within Germany. But German emigrants exported their brewing tradition around the world. They founded Anheuser-Busch in the United States and Tsingtao in China. By the time I opened my business in 1995, homogenous industrial light lager dominated the commercial beer landscape worldwide.

The Reinheitsgebot has endured because you can make great beers with the four core ingredients. But you can't make many of the world's boundlessly exotic and adventurous beers by sticking solely with the four ingredients. I am happy that Germany's beer purity law exists. Because if it didn't, I would not have had something so monolithic and overarching to rebel against when I started Dogfish Head Craft Brewery.

PREFACE

BY TODD AND JASON ALSTRÖM

WHAT`S EXTREME BEER? IT`S A QUESTION THAT WE`RE OFTEN ASKED, BUT FIRST, LET`S TAKE A STEP BACK.

We didn't know it at the time, but we cut our brewing teeth on extreme beer way back in the early '90s at our parents' house in the hills of Monson, Massachusetts. The goal was to create a strong Brown Ale using an old-school LME (liquid malt extract) homebrew kit and a ton of sugar. But we had no freagin' idea what we were doing and wound up raiding the cabinets for every type of sugar we could find. If it was sweet and fermentable (and you name it, from granulated white sugar, to brown sugar, honey, and more), it found its way into our makeshift brew kettle. The result was a skull splitting 14 percent alcohol by volume (ABV) Brown Ale. Extreme? Um, hell yeah!

Soon after, Jason moved to Savannah, Georgia. where his beer world was turned upside down thanks to an archaic alcohol cap that restricted brewers to 6 percent ABV and under at the time. He knew the only way around this obstacle was to continue to brew his own beer. So he did, and his love for bigger, English styles along with a growing affection for American hops gave birth to big, hoppy 7 to 10 percent ABV IPAs. Jason continued to push the limits with homebrewing while he was in Georgia and found even more inspiration in grains and spices from local ethnic grocery stores.

In 1996, we found ourselves living literally two houses away from each other on the shores of East Boston. We were completely infatuated with homebrewing and the rise of the American brewer and brewed furiously every week. For the most part, we stuck to the classic styles of Europe to hone our skills, but we began to twist things in an extreme direction by utilizing interesting fruits, coffee, and other odd adjuncts. And we added reviews to our homebrew notes so we could learn more from batch to batch, applying the same reviewing process to commercial beers soon after. Then, Todd busted out his code ninja skills and began publishing our reviews online. BeerAdvocate was born.

Eight years and many beers later, all of this would inspire us to host our first Extreme Beer Fest in Boston, Massachusetts, on January 17, 2004. It was an event "dedicated exclusively to showcasing beers that push the boundaries of brewing." And it was epic—Legendary, even. It quickly became our signature event and typically sells out in minutes.

In 2008, we asked our friend Sam Calagione at Dogfish Head to become its sponsor as Dogfish Head's off-centeredness and our extreme beer attitude were a perfect pairing. Together, we brewed our first collaborative beer for the 2009 Extreme Beer Fest on Dogfish Head's old-school brewhouse in Rehoboth Beach, Delaware, and have continued the annual tradition ever since. Since we don't get to brew as much as we did back in the day, it helps to keep us grounded.

It's a cool story, but what's extreme beer?!?

As we defined it back in 2003, during our Extreme Beer Fest planning meetings, extreme beer [noun] is a beer that pushes the boundaries of brewing.

That's it. It's a highly flexible definition for beers that defy all current style guidelines and alter our ideas about what we think beer is, should be, and could be.

Before 2002, use of the adjective was pretty much nonexistent. And while it's been documented that Jim Koch of the Boston Beer Co. first used the term to describe Sam Adams Triple Bock, a beer, which, when it was released in 1994 was then the strongest available at 17.5% ABV, few would use the word again until the rise of Double (or Imperial) Stouts and India Pale Ales in the early 2000s. The ensuing battle to shred palates with hops and soak them in booziness would dominate the beer geek scene for years to come, and unfortunately, mainstream media quickly associated extreme beer exclusively with two things: high alcohol and over-the-top hoppy beers.

Not that they were wrong, exactly, but they were only focusing on the surface. Beneath these hyped-up beer styles and fluffy journalism was a concept that's been part of the very fabric of brewing beer since its inception: creativity. We're talking about beers that modify established styles with exotic ingredients or employ new and forgotten brewing and conditioning techniques. We're talking about exciting emerging styles and the mystery of what innovative brewers will give us next. Furthermore, extreme literally means that which exceeds the ordinary, usual, or expected. It's an apropos descriptor for a beer that raises a fist at the norm, especially

the bland, mass-marketed beer that still dominates shelves and consumer palates today. Pair the word with beer and you've got a term that piques interest, generates excitement, immediately raises the bar, and definitely rubs some people the wrong way. Sometimes though, wrong is right. And sure, extreme beer, like any other beer, has seen its share of gimmickry. But today, there's a lot more finesse behind the concept, and some of the best extreme beers are well-balanced, highly drinkable, and moderate in alcohol.

Love or hate it, there's no doubt in our minds that the greater concept of extreme beer is what keeps beer interesting. And that's exactly what this book is about. The countless brewers who continue to inspire us with their creativity—From smacking our palates down with big, bold flavors in the '90s to today's exotic ingredients and imaginative nuances that we've never tasted before.

Speaking of inspiration, during Boston's Extreme Beer Fest in 2015, we teamed up with Sam to begin curating a collection of creative recipes and thoughts on extreme brewing from some of our favorite brewers. The end result of our effort is this book in your hands. In addition to dozens of recipes from our friends, we've also included several of our own extreme beer recipes from past collaborations with Sam and his team at Dogfish Head. We hope you dig 'em.

Thanks for reading and joining us in raising a fist at the norm. Happy (extreme) brewing!

Respect Beer®.

Jason & Todd Alström, founders, BeerAdvocate

PART 1
GETTING
STARTED

 Whether or not you have attempted to homebrew before, it's important to grasp the basics of brewing ingredients and processes before moving ahead, attempting recipes from this book or elsewhere. As things become clearer, your comfort level with the practical aspects of brewing will increase. And as you gain confidence, you'll be more capable of embracing less traditional methods and ingredients. In short, before you can successfully take beer in a new direction, you need to understand exactly what goes into it and become familiar with the tools that are necessary to make it.

CHAPTER 1
INGREDIENTS

Adding yeast to the carboy is the catalyst for fermentation.

There is a seemingly limitless selection of commercially available beers on the market today, from light lagers to dark stouts and from tart wheat beers to roasty porters. But why not make your own? Basically, anyone who can cook a good soup can make a halfway decent beer. Like any art form, brewing affords you, the "cook," the opportunity for some artistic self-expression. The art of brewing begins with the selection of ingredients.

Just as a painter uses different oils, watercolors, and charcoals, the ingredients that go into brewing allow you to express your vision of the perfect pint.

To the uninitiated, it may seem that brewing is a complicated scientific process. In a way, it is; the conversion of starches and carbohydrates to sugars and the subsequent conversion of sugars to alcohol are chemical processes. However, just because there is some basic science going on while the brewing protocols are being followed doesn't mean that making beer needs to be a complicated endeavor. This chapter will demystify both the ingredients and the process.

THE BIG FOUR

Barley, hops, water, and yeast are the primary constituents of almost all beers. Barley, a cereal grain rich in starch, is a prime source of sugar and gives the beer "body" due to its gluten and protein content. Hops, a type of plant grown worldwide and used primarily for beer making, adds flavor and bitterness to counterbalance the sweetness of malt, while also acting as a preservative. Together, barley and hops add "color" to the final product.

Yeast contributes some flavor and aroma to beer, but its primary function is as a catalyst for the fermentation process. Yeast eats the sugar from the barley (or any additional sugar source) and converts that sugar into alcohol. It's as simple as that.

Whether you choose to order your ingredients from a catalog, an online retailer, or your local homebrew store, quality is the number one priority when seeking out ingredients.

BARLEY

Barley is grown all over the world. Brewing barley begins as a seed within a husk. Both unmalted barley and malted barley appear the same in their grain forms. Malted barley is soft enough to be cracked between your teeth. Unmalted barley is very hard, and the starches within are not readily accessible.

The process of malting barley and wheat is fairly complicated and best left to the pros—you needn't convert your spare bedroom into a floor-malting facility in order to make good beer. To malt barley, a maltster (someone who works at a barley malting facility) creates a warm and wet artificial growing environment so that the seeds will think they have been planted in the soil. The barley is first piled up in mounds and then sprayed with water until germination commences. When the grains begin to sprout, the pile is then spread out to encourage the germination process; during this time, the hard inside of the seed, called the endosperm, changes into a softer carbohydrate substance (starch).

Germination is permitted to proceed to the point where the maximum amount of accessible starch exists within the husks. Once this point has been reached, the sprouted grains are shifted into a kiln to dry, which halts the germination process and toasts the barley. The grain has now been malted. If the grain is kilned or dried at lower temperatures, it will be relatively light in shade and contribute less color to your beer. Darker malts, like those used to make stouts, porters, and bocks, are kilned at higher temperatures.

Commercial breweries use vessels called mash tuns to combine hot water with varieties of milled malted barley (and sometimes wheat) in different volumes for different recipes. First, the milled malted barley and warm water are mixed in the mash tun. This mixture is brought to a stable temperature at which enzymes convert the starches in the barley into sugars that will then be available for fermentation. The bottom of the mash tun is perforated like a giant colander. After the grain and water steep like tea for an hour or so, liquid drains out the bottom of the mash tun and is

pumped over to the boil kettle. The grains in the tun are sparged (rinsed) with more warm water to ensure that all of their residual sugars make it into the boil kettle as well. This prefermented beer, known as wort, is then brought to a boil. When you make your own versions of the recipes in this book, you will use prepared malt extract that will allow you to skip the steps of malting, mashing, and sparging. This malt extract was made from partially germinated and then roasted barley.

MALT EXTRACT AND ALL-GRAIN BREWING

Most recipes in this book use small volumes of specialty and dark grains in the same way that a commercial brewer would, but the bulk of the barley source will come from the extract base. The malt extract that will be the main source of fermentable sugars in your brew was prepared in a malting facility. The process of making malt extract involves brewing wort and removing water by means of boiling and withdrawing moisture by way of a vacuum. Unfortunately, this intense condensing process robs the syrup of natural compounds in the barley that are conducive to thorough fermentation. Loose translation: The yeast cells that will ultimately eat and ferment the barley sugars prefer all-grain wort over all-extract wort. So, while the potential difference in quality between an all-grain beer and a partial-grain beer is not all that significant, the potential difference between an all-grain beer and an all-extract beer can be much more noticeable. All-grain beers generally taste better, but well-made extract beers can be equal in quality.

The biggest difference between the two methods is evident when making a very light colored beer. The malt extract process tends to darken the sugars some when compared to the yield of a partial-grain batch. As previously mentioned, the older the malt is, the darker it will appear. The malt kits sold at homebrew shops and in catalogs generally have a two-year shelf life. By using some amount of specialty grains in a bag, you are replacing some of the natural compounds that will be absent from your malt extract. A measurement scale called Lovibond often identifies the colors of malts and barleys (e.g., 20 Lovibond). The lower the Lovibond number, the lighter the color.

Malt extract has improved tremendously for the homebrewer over the last twenty years. In the past, it was mainly produced for commercial bakers. When malted, it was mashed for maximum sugar content, independent of what flavor profile that gave the homebrewer. Nowadays, most malt extract producers make it with brewing in mind and use no coloring agents and a variety of different base malts, which allows the extract brewers to make a wider and more authentic variety of beers. In addition, you can now find extract sold in different packaging from 3 pounds to 9 pounds (1.4 to 4 kg) or bigger packages, allowing the homebrewer to not have to supplement with other sugars to get their gravity where they want it to be.

Other grains: Malt extract is a "base malt" that will be most of the malt in the beer; however, most beers use specialty grains to add mouthfeel, color, sweetness, acidic, etc. These specialty grains are typically used in small percentages of overall malt for the recipe and are added in the steeping process. Mouthfeel or body malts such as carapils (dextrin powder works better for extract), melanoiden, acidulated malts, and a variety of cara (CaraHell, CaraFoam, CaraAroma, and CaraBelge) add fullness or mouthfeel to our beers and will usually help with foam retention in the final product. Crystal (caramel) malts also add to mouthfeel and head retention but predominantly add sweetness and nuttiness as well as caramel and toffee notes, while adding varying degrees of reddish/copper colors. Roasted malts such as Chocolate malt, Black Roasted Barely, and Carafa impart dark colors and flavors such as roasted coffee and bittersweet chocolate. Finally, specialty malts add very unique characteristics: such as Honey malt lending a very sweet honey-like flavor and smoked grains like Peated, Rauch, and a variety of wood smoked malts that, in very small quantities, add pleasant characters to some beers.

Hops can be grown in almost all zones and regions of the world. In the United States, the growing conditions in Washington are ideal for hops. Hop rhizomes typically are sold in late March to early April; however, many places will do an advance sale. To find out if growing hops at home will work for you, either talk to your local homebrew shop or try searching online.

HOPS

Without hops, all beers would be cloyingly sweet. Hop vines grow well in many different regions of the world, but only produce healthy cones within certain latitudes. In its natural state, a hop flower looks like a miniature, soft, green pinecone. If you rub a few fresh hop flowers between your hands, you'll notice that your palms will immediately get tacky. Inside the hop cones are the sticky resins and oils that are most abundant at harvest time. After harvest, the hop cones are laid out and dried until the majority of moisture has been wicked from the flowers in order to allow them to age without spoiling. There is a fine line between drying the hops too much, (which robs them of their flavor and aroma enhancing properties) and not drying them enough (which will cause them to go bad). Once the hops are properly dried, they are either vacuum-packed whole or condensed into pellets and vacuum-packed to await their journey to home and commercial breweries.

The most common vessel in which brewers use their hops is the brew pot (at home) or the boil kettle (at a commercial brewery). The earlier that the hops are added in the boil, the more they will contribute bitterness to the taste of the beer. The later in the boil that the hops are added, the more they will contribute to the aroma of the beer. Most hops will be listed for their intended usage—some hops can span multiple uses, but you will often see recipes refer to bittering hops, aroma hops, and flavoring hops, which also correspond to how long they are used in the boil.

At last check, we found over 170 varietals of hop, and that number is growing rapidly as hop growers are cross-breeding and experimenting to keep pace with the experimental brewing renaissance. Of those 170-plus varieties, about 60 are commonly found in brewing, allowing for a tremendous amount of variation in flavors. Certain hops such as Simcoe, Citra, and Mosaic have become so popular that there is simply not enough of it grown yet to satisfy all the demands of the brewers. Most of the time, you can find substitutes for them—but hold tight, farmers will catch up and they will become available.

Many brewers play around with adding hops post-boil on the way to the fermenting tank or carboy (a large, usually glass, jug-like container generally used to ferment and age beer) or even in the fermenting tank and carboy. This is called dry hopping. Once the boil is over and the wort has settled, it is ready to be chilled and transferred to a fermentation tank or carboy. The temperature at which it should ferment depends on the type of beer that is being made from the wort. If a lager yeast is going to be used, the beer will be transferred at around 45°F (7.2°C) for fermentation. If an ale yeast is going to be used, it will be transferred at about 70°F (21°C) for fermentation.

Hops should be stored cold and oxygen free. Most of the hops you buy will use an oxygen barrier bag. Simply cut open the bag and remove what you need and then push air out of bag, roll it up again, tape it shut, and store it in the freezer.

DRY HOPPING

VINNIE CILURZO, RUSSIAN RIVER BREWING COMPANY

There are six important components to dry hopping: quantity, time, temperature, mixing, multiple dry hop additions, and yeast contact.

1. QUANTITY

At Russian River, on average we dry hop at a rate of 1 pound (455 g) to 2 pounds (900 g) per barrel (31 gallons [117 L]) of beer. This is the equivalent of ¼ ounce (7 g) to 1 ounce (28 g) of dry hops per gallon of homebrew. The amount of dry hops you add to the primary or secondary fermenter depends on how aromatic you want your beer to be. There is no formula to figure out ahead of time to determine what the end aroma will be in your finished beer; this is strictly trial and error. I can give you some broad guidelines, but this is really something that is subjective—a big enough aroma for you may not be enough for me. It is my opinion that aroma is one of the most important components of an IPA or a Double IPA. On average, I go with ½ ounce (15 g) per gallon (3.8 L). When we use an ounce (28 g) per gallon (3.8 L), it is made via multiple dry hop additions over a four-week period. In most cases, we use pelletized hops rather than whole leaf hops to dry hop with. If you are a beginning brewer, you'll definitely want to use pellets. However, as you progress and gain more confidence, you can begin to experiment with hop cones. Using pelletized hops gives you a quicker release of hop oils, whereas dry hopping with hop cones gives you a slower release of their oils and a more subtle hop aroma.

2. TIME

The second point to consider is time. Again, there is no formula for this, and only continued experimentation will yield you useful knowledge for future brews. I like to dry hop our standard Russian River IPA for seven days, our Blind Pig IPA for ten days, our two Double IPAs (Pliny the Elder and HopFather) for twelve to fourteen days, and our Triple IPA (Pliny the Younger) for four weeks. Regardless of how long you dry hop, one of the most important things you can do for making a quality beer is to keep a carbon dioxide blanket on top of your beer in the primary or secondary fermenter. If you are an advanced homebrewer, you may have a CO_2 tank from your draft keg system. But, if you are a beginning brewer, all you need to do to keep the fermentation lock floating gently and rock the fermenter for a few seconds. This will release some CO_2 out of the beer and into the headspace of your fermenter. This is especially important if you are dry hopping your beer in a plastic bucket, as they don't seal as well as glass carboys. If the inside plastic piece of the fermentation lock isn't floating, there probably isn't a good CO_2 blanket in the fermenter. Also, remember that since your homebrew will be sitting for an extended period of time, it's important to keep the light out. If you're aging the beer in a glass carboy, cover it with a large, black plastic trash bag. Light and hops don't mix; when beer comes in contact with light, even for just a few minutes, it creates a skunky flavor. In order to keep an eye on the CO_2 blanket on the beer, try cutting a small hole in the top of the trash bag for the fermentation lock to fit through.

3. TEMPERATURE

For most homebrewers, temperature is not a problem since the beer will be sitting at room temperature. In my opinion, dry hopping between 52°F and 72°F (11°C and 22°C) is critical to getting a big hop aroma in your beer. If the beer is any colder, you won't get as much hop oil extracted into your brew.

4. MIXING

The idea of mixing, or rousing, the dry hops back into the beer during aging is new even to many professional brewers. At Russian River, to drive the dry hops back up into the beer, we push carbon dioxide through the bottom of the tank. This effectively puts the hops back in suspension. For homebrewing, you can actually accomplish this simply by rocking the fermenter gently. This will get the hops back to floating in the beer, thus giving them more contact time. I like to do this five days before the beer will be transferred off the dry hops.

5. MULTIPLE DRY HOP ADDITIONS

Another idea that is new to many professional brewers, and is most certainly considered extreme, is multiple dry hop additions. In most cases, I add a second dry hopping at the same time that we push the initial dry hops back into the beer, five days before the beer is transferred off the dry hops. The one exception is our Triple IPA (Pliny the Younger), which gets four separate dry hops additions. Two weeks after primary fermentation, I add the first dry hop addition. After the initial dry hop, I continue to add the next two dry hop additions in one-week intervals. The final dry hop addition takes place in the serving tank at our brewpub. If you are bottling your homebrew, just give it one more week in the fermenter with the fourth addition. I'd suggest ½ ounce (15 g) per addition; sometimes, less is more when dry hopping.

6. YEAST CONTACT

The sixth and final decision you will need to make when dry hopping is whether to transfer your beer to a secondary fermenter after primary fermentation. This will get your homebrew off the yeast. I find that the more yeast I can remove from the beer before I add the dry hops, the more hop aroma my finished beer will have. With more yeast removed, the hops will have more surface area in contact with the beer to extract more hop oil. These oils will give your beer a big, rich hop aroma.

After more than twenty years of brewing both at home and professionally, I still continue to experiment when it comes to dry hopping. It is one of the most elusive aspects of brewing, but also one of the most enjoyable parts.

WATER

In terms of proportion and volume, water is the main ingredient in beer, yet the importance of it is rarely touched upon in brewing recipes. When you add hops to your beer, you know you are adding only hops and it's relatively easy to estimate the effect that the volume and type of hops being added will have. Water is a little murkier, so to speak. Almost all natural water supplies (municipal, spring, etc.) will have different levels of ions, minerals, gases, and even potential pollutants. Municipal water supplies may even have residual levels of chlorine that retard the fermentation process. However, odds are that if your municipal water supply is fine for drinking, it's fine for homebrewing.

The ideal profile of water is pretty broadly defined; you are basically looking for soft, bacteria-free water that will work well for brewing, cleaning, and sanitizing. As is the case with commercial brewing, you will use a lot more water in the homebrewing process for cleaning and rinsing than for the actual brewing. Most municipal water sources provide clean water that will generally be adequate for homebrewing.

There are several ways to find out more about your water. If you pay a water bill to the town, give the water resource authorities a call. They are required to supply you with an accurate analysis of the water they provide. If you obtain your water from a well, then you will have to pay to get it analyzed by a water quality laboratory. The local government (county, township, extension office, etc.) usually has some listings for private water testing. Search online for one of these or look up a water-treatment equipment company. If you want to do some basic water chemistry, consider using a BrewLab kit by LaMotte, which allows you to not only test your water but to help you alter it as well.

If a company sells water-treatment equipment, they are usually prepared to test your water for free. You can also discuss the water quality with other homebrewers and homebrew supply store workers who have probably already considered the effects of a given water source's profile on different styles of beer.

There are two basic choices with your water supply, provided it is potable and odorless. You either use it the way it is, or you change it to meet your brewing needs. Your choice will likely depend on how technically involved you want to get with your brewing. Some homebrewers do a little of each—they mostly use the water they have and add a tablespoon of gypsum (a mineral consisting of hydrous calcium sulfate) or a pack of water salts (calcium compounds also known as brewing salts) to replicate certain traditional brewing styles.

Another adjustment that can be made to improve the water would be to remove any residual chlorine. This is a fairly easy process. Boiling will remove some of it, but carbon filtration works better and more thoroughly. Activated carbon water filters are so popular for drinking water now that they can be found in many grocery stores as well as big box retailers or specialty stores. Just follow the directions on how to use the activated carbon filter for drinking water and you will have great, dechlorinated water for brewing as well. Many water districts now use chloramines, which cannot be removed by boiling but can be removed with activated carbon or with potassium metabisulfite (campden tablets).

Most of the recipes in this book can be made perfectly with the typical municipal water supply. If your supply is unacceptable, use bottled spring water. If a recipe within this book specifically calls for a necessary water adjustment, it will be clearly marked within the recipe section.

YEAST

Ale and lager yeasts are both from the greater family with the fancy Latin name, *Saccharomyces cerevisiae*. Yeast is technically a fungus (that doesn't sound all that appetizing, does it?). The way yeast cells grow healthy and multiply is by eating sugar, excreting alcohol, and burping CO_2 (come to think of it, that doesn't sound very appetizing either!). This is the crass but easy explanation of the fermentation process.

When it comes to extreme beers, very few things equal the extreme nature of the spontaneously fermented lambic ales of Belgium. These beers hearken back to a time when all beers contained microorganisms that could make them tart and acidic. Louis Pasteur's research on pasteurization showed brewers how to eliminate these wort-spoiling microbes. With this subtraction by elimination, beer changed and began to more closely resemble the beers we consume today. The lambic family of beers remains a remnant of these pre-Pasteur beers, and the method of producing lambics is now a protected appellation. This appellation requires that lambic wort be made from no less than 30 percent unmalted barley and it must undergo spontaneous fermentation for the production of alcohol in the finished beer.

In a little over twenty years, yeast variety for homebrewers has gone from mostly dry packets of limited variety, potentially slightly contaminated yeast to a huge selection of quality dry and liquid cultures with many, many strains to choose from. Liquid cultures of yeast are grown in laboratories and tested to be sure they are bacteria and wild yeast free. These usually come in easy-to-use packaging in the greatest amount of strains available. There are two main manufacturers, Wyeast and White Labs, and several more regional companies popping up to serve homebrewers. Dry yeast historically had potential wild yeast and bacteria during the drying process; however, Lallemand and Fermentis (Safale, Saflager, etc.) have modernized the drying process, essentially removing this issue. Dry yeast is extremely shelf stable and now comes in most of the popular strains.

OTHER INGREDIENTS

In addition to the big four, many beers utilize other ingredients to create unique flavors. These are often added at the end of the boil or in the fermentation stages so to not accidently introduce bacteria or wild yeasts.

SUGARS

Different types of sugars can be added to enhance flavors as well as potentially increase alcohol without increasing residual sweetness. A very popular sugar is candi sugar, which comes in varying colors as well as in crystalline form. Soft sugars and syrups are most commonly used in Belgian-style beers but people are exploring and a few companies are now selling flavored ones like tart cherry, blood orange, Thai ginger, cacao nibs, and more. Demerara sugar is very popular in that it is highly fermentable, allowing people to boost alcohol without boosting flavors. Cane and corn sugars are also commonly used to do that. Honey is often used to enhance delicate flavors and is also highly fermentable. Fruits from apricots to watermelons can be used to flavor beer, and these can be added as fresh fruit, pureed fruit, or added as flavorings.

SPICES/FLAVORS

Common flavors and spices added to beers are vanilla beans, orange peel, coriander, grains of paradise, liquorice root, cacao nibs, hazelnut, and many more. These are typically found as dried products that are used near the end of the boil or are sold as as extracts/flavorings that can even be used in fermentation/bottling.

OAK

While a traditional barrel might not be practical for the homebrewer, there are many easy ways to add oak flavors. Most people add cubes, chips, balls, dust, or extracts to the fermentation process—the longer you leave it in contact, the more the flavors come through.

OTHER

There are a lot of cool and crazy fun things to try adding to beer, some of which haven't even been experimented with yet. One last thing worth noting is the clarity of the final product (when appropriate) can have a significant flavor impact and thusly clarifiers should be considered when making recipes. While the clarifier won't/shouldn't have a flavor itself, the proteins and hazes it keeps out of the final product will help all of your other flavors come through.

This is a healthy yeast head on a fermenting batch of ale.

CONCLUSION

This simple overview of the ingredients and brewing process is the framework from which all recipes in this book will be executed. Extreme beers are beers with nontraditional ingredients or traditional ingredients added in exaggerated amounts. Most of the recipes in this book are extreme to one degree or another (more than a few are extreme in both ways). While making an extreme beer might add a step (or three) to the process, believe me when I say that if the brewing process outlined in this chapter makes sense, then the additional steps that have been added for certain brews will be just as easy to comprehend and perform. Making good beer is a skill. Making exceptional beer is an art form. While you may not be ready to wear a beret just yet, the goal here is to make you an artist in no time.

CHAPTER 2 EQUIPPING YOUR HOME BREWERY

A clean carboy is essential to homebrewing; sterilize your carboy prior to use by agitating with sanitizer and warm water.

In homebrewing, as in any hobby, the process can be as simple or as complicated as you make it. Of course, the more complicated you decide to make the process, the more equipment you will need. By focusing on recipes that call for malt extract as the malt sugar source, the full-scale mashing step can be skipped. Eliminating this step will save you not only time on your brew day, but also money, as you won't need to purchase the necessary mashing equipment.

Another factor that will determine how much equipment you'll need is knowing how often you're planning to brew. Most of the recipes in this book are for ales. Ales usually take a shorter time to make than lagers. Since so many of these recipes are for beers that are stronger than the average commercial varieties, they require extended fermenting and conditioning time. The actual time it takes to brew a batch of beer is fewer than four hours. However, with fermentation, aging, bottling, and bottle-conditioning (the time required to build up the desired level of carbonation in the bottle), there will be a turnaround time of about a month before all of your equipment is freed up to brew the next batch. If you plan to brew more frequently than this, you will need an extra carboy or two, extra bottles, and at least twice as much storage space.

A recent trend in brewing is changing the traditional batch size, which historically has been 5 gallons (19 L). The batch size doesn't usually alter the time it takes to make/age a beer, so some brewers who use a more complicated process will produce larger batches 10–20 gallons (38–76 L) to maximize their time. While others who don't want a large amount of beer around or for whom space is an issue may opt for a smaller batch size. Either way, there are now a plethora of options to either start at any size or to scale up or down with much of the same equipment.

WHERE TO BUY EQUIPMENT

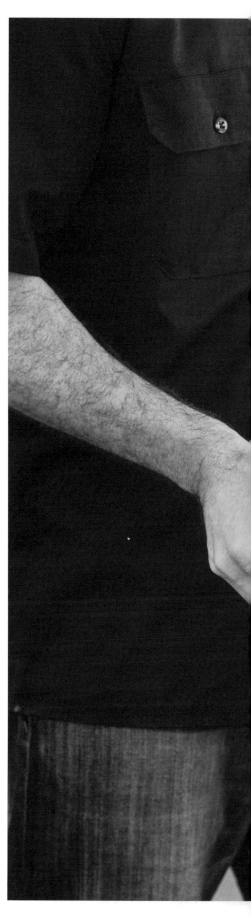

A key factor to your brewing success is often the resources you have access to when first starting out. If you have a good local homebrew supply store, then that is often your best way to go. This gives you the ability to ask questions, get product walk throughs, and these often provide beginning brewing classes. A new brewer may want to check out online marketplaces before going into their local homebrew store or if they don't have one convenient to them. The competitive online marketplace has really driven down prices for new brewers. The standard "starter kit" is extremely affordable and usually has lots of options from bare bones and inexpensive all the way up to all grain and kegging kits.

Beyond just the stores where homebrewing supplies are purchased, the new brewer often has access to clubs of other fanatical brewers in their area. Clubs are a great way to get knowledge quickly and to have people sample and give feedback on your beer. And they typically host events centered around this great hobby. Search online for homebrew clubs in your area.

SANITIZING YOUR EQUIPMENT

While not a piece of homebrewing equipment per se, what you use to sanitize with and how you do it are major factors in determining the drinkability of your beer. Sanitizing should be the first thing you do when you bring home your new equipment, as countless people most likely have already handled it. A good starter kit should come with a sanitizer that is designed to work on all the materials you use (plastics, glass, and metals). Star San and Iodophor are great sanitizers, and when used correctly, these leave behind no residual taste or odors but are safe to use. Bleach can also be used at 1 tablespoon (15 ml) per gallon (3.8 L) of water, but please do not use it on stainless steel and be sure to rinse your equipment thoroughly after using bleach.

BASIC EQUIPMENT

Chapter three will take you through the step-by-step process of brewing a batch of beer. For the sake of continuity, the equipment you'll need to brew with is listed in the same order as it is used in chapter 3: Making Your First Batch of Beer, (page 44).

Here's all the equipment you will need to take your beer from the brew pot, through fermentation, and into the bottle:

A Carboy (without accessories)

B Carboy with stopper and airlock on top

C Bottling bucket

D Bottle/transfer tubing

E Capper

F Hydrometer and test vial

G Bottle filter

H Bottle brush

I Siphon setup

J Intro book

K PBW cleaner

L Starsan Sanitizer

M Funnel

N Sample taker

O Stirring spoon

P Thermometer

Q Specialty grain bag and hops bag

R Wort chiller

STIRRING SPOON

You will want to have a good long spoon made from either stainless steel or rigid, unmeltable plastic. Wood is all right to use during the boil, but remember that wood is porous and an excellent home for beer-spoiling bacteria. The design of the spoon should be as simple as possible. An ornate, grooved spoon or one stamped with a funky design might look nice, but any grooves, nooks, or crannies are only going to make sanitization that much more difficult.

The length of the handle is most easily determined by considering the height of the brew pot's sidewall. The handle of the spoon should be a good foot (30 cm) longer than the pot's height. A well-brewed beer is one that's made with a vigorous boil. There is nothing worse than being burned by the splash of boiling beer that can occur when you are adding hops or other ingredients to the boil. There is less chance of this happening if your stirring spoon has a nice long handle.

BREW POT

Of all the equipment you'll need for homebrewing, the brew pot may be the biggest expense. However, a good boil kettle will not only make your brew day easier, but it also plays a big role in the flavor and repeatability of your beer. Key things to look for are material and size. Doing a full volume boil (meaning if you're making 5-gallon [19 L] batch you start with 6+ gallons [23+ L]) is ideal, as the sugars will be fully diluted in the boil. This not only ensures all the liquid goes through the boil, making it sanitized, but you also end up with lighter colors in the final products as the sugars will caramelize less.

When shopping, look for an oversized, 100 percent stainless steel pot. You will be brewing 5-gallon (19 L) batches, but it's important to have plenty of headroom for accommodating extra ingredients and a vigorous boil. A 7- or 8-gallon (26 or 30 L) pot is ideal. You might be tempted to use inexpensive, porcelain-covered steel or aluminum pots, but don't. With all of the stirring required in making good beer, it's inevitable that the porcelain will eventually chip and the now-exposed cheaper steel will rust and contribute a metallic taste and possibly contaminate your beer. There are many kettles built for homebrewing that come with clad bottoms (for even heat distribution), lots of extra capacity, interior volume markers (for easy measurement), welded or weldless ball valves, and thermometers, as well as notched lids and silicon handle covers. While these are not necessary to make great beer, they make all aspects of the process a little easier and more repeatable.

GOING BIG/CHILLING

Many people choose to use larger brewing kettles so they can make either full volume boils and/or do bigger batches. This choice usually results in the homebrewer either being forced out of the kitchen due to inadequate power from the stove or a spouse/significant other kicking them out due to aroma (which we think is fantastic) or boil over messes. Outdoor burners, often used for frying turkeys, can be found almost anywhere and for little cost. These can really shorten your brewday, as well as let you brew anywhere outside, which means easy cleanup. Also, when boiling over 3–4 gallons (11–15 L), you will need a wort chiller to cool the boil down after. Wort chillers come in a variety of styles, but most new brewers choose immersion chillers, which are copper (or stainless) coils that you put (immerse) into your boil near the end of the boil. After 10–20 minutes of sitting at boiling temperature, they will be fully sanitized, and then you can simply run water to them to chill the beer down before adding the yeast. This fast chilling helps reduce the chances of airborne yeasts and bacteria from spoiling your batch.

THERMOMETER

While you may be tempted to buy a digital-readout probe thermometer at a homebrew supply shop, an inexpensive glass thermometer purchased at any supermarket is just as effective. In my experience, the digital ones can be complicated to use and lose calibration easily. Also, home cooking thermometers don't float and tend to be sturdier. You need the thermometer for properly steeping specialty grains, chilling the beer for appropriate yeast-pitching temperatures, and monitoring fermentation temperatures, so it's really not a good idea to skimp on a simple piece of equipment that is this critical. A wide range of easy to use and effective thermometers have appeared in recent years, including a liquid crystal style that attaches to the outside of the vessel and clip-on dial thermometers for the brew pot.

SPECIALTY GRAIN BAG

Specialty grain bags are the extreme brewer's best friend. They are little cheesecloth or nylon bags that hold about 1 pound (455 g) or so of specialty grains. Specialty grains can be steeped without a bag, but then you'll need to use a tight colander or some other means of straining out the barley solids after the steeping is complete. It's much easier to use these inexpensive bags that can be found in any good homebrew supply source. Look for the kind that has a drawstring closure on the top to keep the grains from floating out. Basically, they're like giant tea bags, and you will probably get a few uses out of one drawstring bag before it falls apart. If these aren't available, make sure the bag is big enough to hold the grain needed for the recipe and that there's enough material left at the top of the bag to tightly knot and seal. The cheesecloth bags are cheap enough that it won't be too painful to your wallet to use them once and throw them out.

You may also use the specialty grain bags to occasionally hold whole leaf hops, spices, or herbs. Hop pellets break into small particles easily enough that they can be added freely to the boil or fermented when the recipes calls for them. Whole leaf hops, however, can

get pretty messy and block the flow of beer from the brew pot to the carboy or from the carboy to the bottling bucket. By packing the whole leaf hops into a cheesecloth sack, they will be much easier to use, remove from the beer, and dispose of. It is important not to pack the sacks too tightly as the hops will expand when wet. To fully absorb the goodness of the hops, the whole sack should be soaked through by the beer.

CAN OPENER

Depending on your source of malt extract, a basic can opener will be needed to open canned malt extract.

them have gone down dramatically as of late. These are great tools as you can get gravity readings with only a few drops of liquid. If you want to use one now or in the future, it is recommended that you do some extra reading on them and potentially use brewing software to help with corrections, especially any done after fermentation has started.

FUNNEL

If your kettle doesn't have a ball valve, then a funnel will be needed to transfer the beer from the brew pot to the glass carboy at the end of your brew day. It's best to use a funnel with a thin enough neck to sit comfortably and securely into the top opening of your carboy. A good funnel is made of food-grade plastic and is usually between 8 inches (20 cm) and 1 foot (30 cm) in diameter at its widest point.

HYDROMETER AND TEST VIAL

This is one of the most critical tools for properly making beer at home. A hydrometer measures the amount of sugar in the beer by measuring the specific gravity. It bobs in a test vial and is marked along its neck in a similar way that a thermometer is marked. As the yeast eats the sugars and converts them to alcohol, there will be fewer sugars in the solution, which lowers the specific gravity of the beer. The higher the specific gravity of the beer, the higher the hydrometer floats in the vial. The lower the specific gravity, the deeper the hydrometer will be submerged in the beer. The hydrometer is used on brew day to make sure that the original target specific gravity has been hit. It's also used to test the beer as it ferments so that you will know when it hits the desired final specific gravity. You are best off buying a hydrometer from a trusted homebrew supply source. Make sure it's properly calibrated for testing beer, as different hydrometers are used in different industries. The test vial can be purchased either with or separately from the hydrometer. As the hydrometer is made of glass, it's best to store it within the vial somewhere safe when it's not in use. While you can get glass vials, I recommend getting one made from food-grade plastic as the glass vials can break pretty easily as well. Refractometers have grown in popularity for homebrewers, especially as prices for

CARBOY

Using a glass or PET carboy for fermentation is a simple yet worthwhile upgrade to invest in. Most turnkey, start-up homebrew kits come with two food-grade 5- to 8-gallon (19 to 30 L) buckets for fermenting and another one for bottling. The plastic fermenters work fine but can be difficult to clean as they have a flat bottom and the plastic is usually more porous than a glass carboy. Rarely, when using ingredients that are larger than the opening of the carboy, plastic buckets actually work better because of their large openings. At a minimum, the carboy should be large enough to yield 5-gallon (19 L) batches, though it's really best to use a 6- or 6½-gallon (23 or 25 L) glass carboy so that there is plenty of space in the top for vigorously fermenting strong batches of beer. Many types of plastic are permeable by oxygen. However, a newer type of carboy made from a plastic called PET (polyethylene terephthalate) has recently been introduced to the homebrewer. PET plastic is acceptable for homebrewing as it's not permeable by oxygen. PET carboys are lightweight (1½ pounds [680 g] versus over 14 pounds [6.4 kg] for a 6½-gallon [25 L] carboy), they won't break, and they have a larger opening than glass carboys. Before brewing, fill your carboy with water poured from a gallon jug so that you can use tape to mark the targeted 5-gallon (19 L) point on the outside of the carboy. The more sugar added during fermentation, whether fruit purée, brown sugar, or anything else, the more the yeast will multiply and the more space you'll need to accommodate yeast growth and the additional ingredients themselves.

Whether you use a bucket or a carboy for primary fermentation, you'll need a glass or PET plastic carboy, sized to your batch of beer, (usually 5 gallons [19 L]), if you plan to secondary ferment. Secondary fermentation is more about storing the beer for dry hopping and clarification than about actual fermentation. This is also a good way to store your beer if you find you don't have time to bottle it. I like to get the beer out of the bucket within two weeks of the start of fermentation. The beer can be racked to a secondary fermentation vessel any time after most of the fermentation has been completed (4 to 7 days after start of fermentation). Visually, you'll notice the foam head of an ale will star to fall, or if you use a hydrometer, you'll notice the gravity has dropped more than ¾ of the way from

starting to finish gravity. After racking the beer to the carboy and adding any dry hops, if needed, the carboy should be topped off with water to be within 4 inches (10 cm) of the top to reduce oxidation. Little air will be left at the top of the carboy. A stopper and airlock must be fitted to the carboy to keep it from getting contaminated and releasing any CO_2.

While not necessary, it's nice to have two carboys so that you can transfer the beer out of the first one and let it age a bit in the second. The primary fermenting carboy will have a lot of proteins and spent yeast cells that will settle to the bottom after fermentation. It helps to remove the beer from these solids if you plan to age it for an extended period of time before bottling.

STOPPER AND AIRLOCK

For most of the buckets designed for homebrewing, you will need only an airlock. The bucket lid will come with a hole that is fitted with a rubber gasket into which the airlock will fit snuggly. Some buckets come with a large hole that requires a stopper, and all carboys require a stopper. The rubber stopper has a similar hole on top and is sized to fit tightly in the neck of a standard carboy. There are a few common designs for airlocks that can be bought from any homebrew supply source; they all work well and are around the same price. The airlock allows the beer to ferment safely, without exposing it to any potential airborne contaminants. As the yeast eats the sugars and converts them to alcohol, the byproduct, CO_2, needs to escape. If the fermenter was sealed, the gas would have nowhere to go and the pressure buildup would eventually break the fermenter. The airlock has space for water within its chamber so that the gas can bubble through without exposing the beer in the fermenter to air. You can also use grain alcohol or vodka in the airlock to make sure the liquid can't grow bacteria, but boiled or distilled sterile water works fine, too.

SIPHON SETUP

This setup will be used to transfer the beer from the carboy into the bottling bucket and then from the bottling bucket into bottles. Look for food-grade, 3/8-inch (1 cm) OD racking cane and 5/16-inch (8 mm) or 3/8 inch (1 cm) tubing (check your homebrew supply source) and make sure it's long enough to do the job properly. It needs to be capable of running from the bottom of a carboy, out the top, and down into the bottom of another carboy with a bit of room to spare. Six or seven feet (approximately 2 m) of hosing should suffice. There is a lot of surface area inside this piece of hose, so make sure it's sufficiently flushed out after using it and well sanitized before using it again. The racking cane should have a footing to keep from pulling sediment from the bottom.

BOTTLE CAPS

Homebrew supply sources offer a few different options for bottle caps. The styles that have a thin, porous, oxygen-scavenging layer on the inside cost a bit more but are worth the price. They will absorb a good amount of the oxygen present in the bottle neck (between the cap and the top of the beer itself), which will improve the taste and shelf life of your beer. If there is a decent-sized craft brewery near you, it can't hurt to ask if they have any extra bottle caps they aren't using and may be willing to part with. Oftentimes, when a brewery changes its cap artwork, they'll end up with cases of the old design that they're willing to part with, sometimes for free. Make sure the caps are sterilized in a solution of hot water just before using them.

CAPPER

There are two standard options for homebrew cappers and both work fine. The cheaper option is the double-lever, hand-held model that gets placed over the top of the bottle when being used. You have to manually hold the cap on the top of the bottle when using this style capper. The more expensive type sits on a little platform and uses a magnet to hold the cap in place. You then place the beer-filled bottle on the center of the platform and pull a lever down to crimp the cap onto the top of the bottle. The cheaper style involves a bit more elbow grease and isn't quite as durable as the second option, but unless you are bottling every day, it should hold up just fine.

While there are a number of bottle cappers available, this style is simple and easy to use.

A specially designed bottle rinser is indispensable for sanitizing your bottles.

BOTTLE BRUSHES

These simple brushes are sized to fit into the necks of bottles so that you can properly clean them out before using them again. Whether you use a brush or not, it's wise to wash out every bottle of beer that you plan to fill with homebrew and then store them in a case box upside down. This will prevent them from getting really cruddy on the bottom. You may want to buy a bottle rinser, which is a device that attaches to most sink spouts and shoots a jet of water into the empty bottle. They don't cost much and are easier to use than a bottle brush, but will work only if your bottles were well rinsed after their last use.

BOTTLING BUCKET

The standard bottling bucket holds at least 5 gallons (19 L) of beer and comes with a plastic valve near its base to which the siphon setup is secured for bottling. You will be filling this bucket with the beer from your carboy just before bottling. Before adding the beer to the bucket, add your sterile-water-diluted priming sugar to ensure predictable carbonation within each bottle. Making sure the whole setup is completely sanitized before use is critical. Don't forget to breakdown the screw-on valve at the base of the bottling bucket and soak all of the parts in sanitizing solution before and after using them.

BOTTLE TREE

You can make a bottle tree yourself but they don't cost that much to buy from homebrew supply sources and they make the bottling process a lot more organized, sanitary, and manageable. As their name suggests, they look like little trees with bare branches that are angled upwards. Once the bottles are cleaned, you place them bottle neck down on the bottle tree. This allows them to drip dry before bottling, and it keeps them in a clean, easy-to-access place. Many bottle trees have a swivel base so you can spin them and pluck the bottles off as needed. Make sure that the branches of the tree have been wiped down with sanitizer prior to bottling as they will be in contact with the inside of your bottles.

BOTTLES

With so many commercial breweries bottling their beer in either clear or green glass for aesthetic purposes, most people assume they are as good an option as old-fashioned brown bottles. This is simply not true. Both green and clear glass allow light to get through the bottle, potentially damaging the beer. Big breweries use preservatives to maximize the shelf life of their beer, but because homebrew is made with all natural ingredients, it's more susceptible to light damage, specifically, a skunky aroma. Therefore, you should always use brown glass.

The most standard size of brown bottle is the 12 ounce (355 ml) longneck favored by so many packaging craft breweries. They are easy to find and easy to use. Be sure to use a bottle that requires a bottle opener as opposed to a twist-off style. The pop-top option gives a much better seal to prevent flat-beer, oxidation, and potentially spoiled beer. Many craft breweries and homebrewers also package in 22 ounce (650 ml) "bomber" bottles or 750 ml (25 ounce) Champagne bottles. They make for a more impressive presentation and are ideally sized for sharing with friends over a meal. More importantly, they hold roughly twice as much beer as a standard 12-ounce (355 ml) bottle, which means you'll be cleaning, filling, and capping half as many bottles needed for a 5-gallon (19 L) batch. Make sure they all take a standard crown cap; some of the European bottles won't. A 5-gallon (19 L) batch will yield slightly more than two cases, or fifty to fifty-five 12-ounce (355 ml) bottles. It's a good idea to clean a few extra bottles to have on hand as you never know when one might slip and break or when your dog might slobber over the top of one and render it unsanitary.

BOTTLE FILLER

Many bottling buckets have a simple valve near the bottom of the sidewall that can either be used alone for bottling or connected to the hose of the siphon setup and bottle filler. The hose and bottle filler method is better. The bottle filler is a rigid food-grade plastic tube that has a valve at the bottom that will stop and start the filling action when it's depressed against the bottom of the bottle. This method allows the bottle to be filled from the bottom up, which is important. This process helps to evacuate unwanted air from the bottle that can lead to oxidation and possible spoilage.

Many resources can be found online to create personalized beer labels at home.

THE FINISHING TOUCH

While it isn't necessary to label your bottles of homebrew, it is fun, easy, and offers the opportunity to further differentiate the beer that you have proudly made from commercial brews.

The easiest way to make quality labels is to use colored paper personalized with your own artwork and verbiage, run off from your home printer. Once the artwork is the right size, you should be able to fit six or eight labels on a standard 8½ x 11 inch (22 x 28 cm) piece of paper. After the labels have been printed, lay them out on newspaper in a well-ventilated area. Spray the front with a film of clear polyurethane. This will protect the label and prevent the artwork from bleeding once the bottle becomes wet. After they're dry, cut out the individual labels and affix them to the clean, finished bottles of homebrew with strong glue.

Once you have purchased all the necessary equipment, take some time to really familiarize yourself with the function of each item before your first brew day. It's only natural to be a bit anxious as you begin the first batch, so it's best not to add to this by trying to learn about the equipment at the same time that your beer is boiling. It's a good idea to set each piece of equipment up in the actual order in which it will be used, as this will cut down on potential confusion. Focus on keeping everything as simple (and sanitized) as possible, and you'll be well on your way to producing your first batch of extremely enjoyable, extreme beer.

Some homebrewers use bottles that still have labels of a big commercial brewer on them. Compared to a clean, unmarked bottle, or those with a homemade label, the bottles that were never cleaned off usually aren't as good. Maybe some fraction of this reality is perception, but the individual who takes the time to personalize and enhance his or her bottle artwork usually takes more effort to personalize and enhance the quality of the beer within that bottle.

THE BOTTLENECK OF BOTTLING

One of the things many homebrewers will admit to is temporarily "quitting" homebrewing because they didn't want to deal with bottling anymore. This isn't usually in the beginning when they are excited about every process, but tasks of peeling old labels off, cleaning, sanitizing, drying, and storing empty and recently filled bottles gets pretty old after a while. Many people turn to kegging their beer in the old soda-style kegs often called "corny's" after a famous brand. These kegs range from 1 to 5 gallons (3.8 to 19 L) and offer the brewer only one vessel to clean and sanitize as well as better carbonation control and the ability to pour small pours when they may not want a full bottle of their beer—especially when sampling young beers while they are maturing.

CHAPTER 3 MAKING YOUR FIRST BATCH OF BEER

There are two parts to any successful beer recipe. This first part lists the ingredients needed to brew the highest-quality beer. The second is the process—the sequence of steps you must take to successfully make a particular beer. This chapter will cover the finer points of both steps. Don't expect your first batch to go perfectly. Though it's perfectly natural to have a little anxiety, it's important to realize that mistakes do happen. But if you take the time to develop a plan that includes gathering ingredients and equipment and then thoroughly read the process before beginning, the odds are really good that you'll be enjoying the fruits of your labor in no time flat. If you are brewing with a friend, use the time it takes to sip a pint together to review the forthcoming day's brew and locate ingredients and equipment.

Whether it's a small batch produced at home or an enormous batch made at a commercial brewery, the actual brewing of the beer takes only a small fraction of the time it takes to ferment and age, which can be anywhere from a week to several months. Ales usually ferment in half the time that lagers do, but the stronger the beer (with more fermentable sugars available for the yeast to eat), the longer it will take to ferment and mature before it's at its optimal quality. You will move your beer into primary fermentation on the same day it is brewed.

GOOD CARPENTERS HAVE ALL OF THEIR TOOLS READY

The first thing to do on brew day is review your equipment and ingredients. Make sure the equipment is clean and in working order and that all of your ingredients are fresh.

EQUIPMENT

Most equipment required to brew beer comes with the turnkey homebrew kits that are sold online or at a neighborhood homebrew supply store. Kits usually include a plastic bucket for fermenting and bottling, as well as other tools. The only upgrades I suggest are a glass or PET carboy, specialty grain sacks, and a bottle tree. The glass or PET carboy will allow you to more easily see how well your beer is fermenting and to know when it is done. Also, they are a lot easier to clean and have less of a chance of contamination than plastic buckets. The most common sizes of carboys used in homebrewing are 5 and 6 gallons (19 and 23 L) and I recommend buying the 6-gallon (23 L) size. While the recipes outlined in this book are designed to yield 5 gallons (19 L) of beer, having a carboy with extra space is a good idea, particularly when brewing strong beers or beers with fruit and other sugars added during fermentation. The extra space will accommodate the extra

yeast growth and vigorous fermentation that takes place when the additional ingredients are introduced, reducing the chance that the beer will ferment out the top of the vessel. Upgrading to specialty grains will allow you to make more diverse styles of beer than if you brewed with extract alone. And, finally, a bottle tree is worth having because it offers a more convenient and sanitary way to prepare and stage your bottles for when the beer is ready to be packaged.

INGREDIENTS

This particular recipe illustrates the extent to which additional sugars can add to the alcohol content and complexity of beer. This batch contains malt extract, steeped specialty grains, hops, water, yeast, KICK Carrageenan Tablet (a clarifying agent), and Belgian candi syrup (beet sugar) that has been infused with coriander and orange. Check the hop pellets to make sure they are fresh and more green than brown. They should disintegrate between the thumb and finger only with great effort. If they are spongy or crumble easily, they are not at their peak. Hops are grown on trellises and are dependent on an ideal growing climate for their quality. Different varieties will contribute different levels of taste and aroma. They are harvested each fall and then processed and shipped. Some hop varieties store better than others, so check with your supplier to determine quality and freshness.

SANITATION

The importance of sanitation cannot be overemphasized; it is the single biggest factor between producing a drinkable beer and one that must be dumped. Yeast is not the only microorganism that likes to eat sugar; bacteria like to eat it too. Like yeast, certain kinds of bacteria will multiply very quickly in a sugar-rich environment. They can overwhelm the yeast and rapidly make your beer sour and undrinkable. Sanitize your equipment by scrubbing the surface of everything with clean water and a cleaning agent such as B-Brite, C-Brite, Easy Clean, or Easy Alkaline (some of the commercial brands developed for brewers), or if clean, simply use Star San or Iodophor. It's always better to err on the side of cleaning too much as opposed to not cleaning enough.

READING THE RECIPE

Starting and final specific gravity and International Bittering Units (IBUs) are key terms that you will see listed at the bottom of each recipe in this book. These measurements have a great effect on the outcome of your finished brew as well as the final alcohol content by volume.

GRAVITY

Gravity is the measurement of how much sugar is in your wort. You measure gravity by using a hydrometer or refractometer. Before the yeast converts the sugar into alcohol, the gravity will be very high. Once the yeast has done its job and there is very little sugar left, the gravity will be low. The gravity before fermenting is called initial or starting gravity and the hydrometer will bob high in its test vial at this point. When you put your finished beer into a clean test vial after fermentation, the hydrometer will sink deep into the liquid. This final measurement is called the terminal or final gravity. Use the alcohol scale on your hydrometer. Subtract your end reading from your initial reading to get your final alcohol content.

Alcohol by volume = Original gravity/0.75

INTERNATIONAL BITTERING UNITS

IBUs are the measured units that brewers use to gauge the level of hop bitterness in beers. Different hops have different alpha acid levels; the more alpha acids a variety of hops have, the more bitterness they will impart on the beer. True bitterness can only be realized by boiling the hops. When you dry hop a beer or add hops post-boil, you will be adding to the hop aroma but not actually upping the IBUs or bitterness substantially.

Gravity and IBU utilization are really the only technical concepts that move the homebrewing experience beyond the normal cooking procedures that any good chef would be faced with in the kitchen. They are not difficult to master, and once you are comfortable with them, you are on the way to being a very competent brewer.

BREWING STEP-BY-STEP

It's now time to start brewing the virgin batch. The pilot brew being made is called Belgian Candi'd Hash. Although the beer will be complex, the brewing process is not—the candi sugar allows these exotic flavors to be infused into your beer without the risk of over/under flavoring it. I promise, if you can drink a beer, you can make this beer. There are twenty-six letters in the alphabet, and there are twenty-six steps in brewing this beer.

Here's an additional note regarding ingredient quantities: Although liquid measurements are typically given in gallons (and liters), liquid malt extract usually comes in large containers that are weighed as pounds (and kilograms). When a recipe calls for a number of pounds (or kilograms) for a liquid ingredient, it is usually referring to the size of the container that it comes in.

A. HEAT THE WATER FOR USE IN THE BREWING PROCESS.

Some of the older homebrewing books recommend boiling the malt extract in 1½ gallons (5.6 L) of water, but this ratio makes for syrupy wort (pre-fermented beer) that can result in unwanted color due to caramelization. Ideally, wort should be thin. The secret is to use a bigger pot—something stainless steel that can hold at least 5 gallons (19 L). The goal is to start with 5 gallons (19 L) of wort and end up with about 4½ gallons (17 L) after the normal evaporation rate during a standard one-hour boil. After adding 4½ gallons (17 L) of cold water to the brew pot, load the crushed crystal specialty grains into the grain bag; knot the opening at the top and place in the cold water. Place the pot on the stove burner and turn burner on high.

B. STEEP THE SPECIALTY GRAINS TO MAKE PREBOIL TEA.

Load the specialty grains into the grain bag. Place the grain bag into the brew pot. As the water temperature increases, your specialty grains' sugars and flavors will start to dissolve. This will give the beer more complexity and depth. Let the grains steep in the brew pot until the water temperature rises to 170°F (77°C). Occasionally, move the grain bag up and down as you would when using a tea bag to make tea. This will help extract more of the flavors and sugars out of the grains.

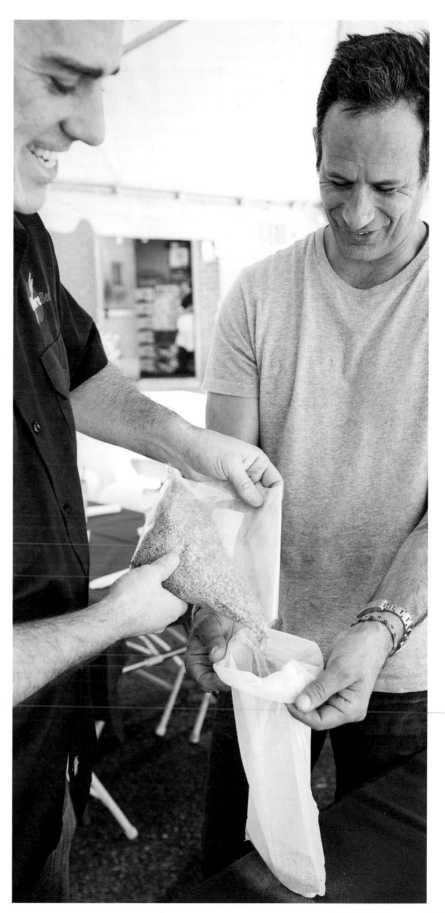

C. REMOVE THE GRAINS AND BRING TO A BOIL.

When the water temperature rises to 170°F (77°C), pull the grain bag out of the brew pot using your stirring spoon and hold it directly above the pot to let most of the water drain from the bag. Do not squeeze the excess water from the grain bag or allow the water temperature to rise above 170°F (77°C) before removing the grain, as these actions will introduce too many tannins into your beer. At this point, you should see the nice color the grain has added as well as its aromas. Feel free to cool off a small spoonful to taste what they will add to your beer as well. Bring the malty water (at this point called wort) up to a boil; once there, turn the heat off.

D. ADD THE MALT EXTRACT.

Next, remove the pot from the heat, add the malt extract to the brew pot, and thoroughly stir to make sure all the malt dissolves. If any malt is left sticking to the bottom of the pot, it has the potential to burn or scorch. Liquid malt extract is thick and syrupy. Most people use some of the hot liquid to get as much of the extract into the kettle; the warm water breaks down the sticky extract.

E. RETURN TO HEAT AND STIR OCCASIONALLY AS THE WORT COMES TO A BOIL.

This will help to break down any clumps of extract that would add unwanted color and reduce the amount of available sugars. Liquid malt extract will cling to the bottom of the pot and may be scorched; removing the pot from the heat and stirring will prevent this from happening.

F. ONCE THE WORT BEGINS TO BOIL, ADD A FEW HOP PELLETS TO THE BOILING LIQUID.

An antifoam agent may also be added. This will help reduce the chance of a boil over. Most of the time, simply lowering the temperature as the foam on top grows is the best way to handle the boil over. Do this repeatedly until it no longer foams excessively.

G. ADD THE MAGNUM HOP PELLETS TO THE BREW POT AFTER BOILING FOR 5 MINUTES.

Stir the boiling wort to help break down the hop pellets and any chunks of malt extract that may have formed. Start timing your 60-minute boil at this hop addition.

Because homebrewers often try to make their beers in smaller pots, they have less-than-ideal headspace to allow for a vigorous boil. A vigorous boil means better hop utilization and better breakdown of all of the added sugars. A bigger brew pot helps.

Keep the bag submerged in the boiling liquid. Just don't forget about your silverware when throwing out the used hop bag at the end of the brew! Submerge the bag of hops into your brew pot 50 minutes into the boil.

H. ADD THE CLARIFYING AGENT.

Add the KICK Carrageenan Tablet, which will act as a clarifying agent for the beer, 40 minutes into the boil. If you are using an immersion chiller, now is a good time to add it so it gets sanitized by the heat of the last 20 minutes of the boil.

I. ADD YOUR CANDI SUGAR.

You may want to turn the heat off when adding your Belgian candi sugar as it is a sugar and is dense—so it might go to the bottom and scorch if not stirred until it is diluted. Add the candi sugar.

Pour the hop pellets into the boiling wort.

J. SHUT OFF THE STOVE BURNER 60 MINUTES INTO THE BOIL.

Remove the brew pot from the heat source.

K. ADD THE HOP HASH.

After the kettle is no longer vigorously boiling, add in your hop hash and stir.

L. CREATE A WHIRLPOOL.

After a minute or so, stir the now-still wort clockwise with a sanitized stirring spoon until you build up a whirlpool effect. This action will help push some of the unwanted solids to the center and bottom of the brew pot. Stir the wort in this manner for 2 minutes and then let the brew pot sit for a bit.

M. COOL YOUR WORT QUICKLY.

There are two easy ways to cool your wort down after the boil: one is use a wort chiller and the other is to make a cold water bath. If you are using an immersion chiller, you would have added it during the boil, and now is time to hook it to a water source and go slowly as that initial water is extremely hot. Also, it's a good idea to use tinfoil to cover up the lid so things can't fall/fly into the cooling wort. Another way to cool wort is to use a water bath. To do this, fill your sink halfway with water and a few trays of ice. Assuming your sink is of ample size, it will act as a cold water bath to cool the wort before transferring it into the glass carboy and pitching the yeast. Carefully set the brew pot in the cold water and let it sit for 30 minutes or so. This is a good time to clean up the mess that is inevitable with homebrewing.

Be careful to cover the brew pot. As the wort temperature drops below 180°F (82°C), it's capable of supporting bacterial growth and you don't want to risk contaminating it. Put the brew pot in a cold water bath in the sink. Change the water as needed to cool the brew pot.

N. TRANSFER THE WORT.

You should calibrate your fermenter ahead of time by filling it with water poured from a 1-gallon (3.8 L) container. This will allow you to mark the exact 5-gallon (19 L) level on the outside of the bucket or carboy with tape or permanent marker. Prepare to transfer the wort from the brew pot to the carboy by putting the carboy on the floor in front of the sink. Either use tubing from a ball valve or put the funnel in the top of carboy. Once the wort temperature falls below 75°F (24°C), it's ready to be transferred. Pour the cooled wort into the carboy using a large funnel. Leave behind in the brew pot as many solids as possible that will have accumulated due to the whirlpool. Allow the wort to splash to aerate the wort and introduce yeast-friendly oxygen.

O. RECORD INITIAL GRAVITY AND MAKE ADJUSTMENTS.

Once the wort is in the fermenter, add cold water, if needed, until the liquid volume of wort is 4½ gallons (18 L). Take a sample of the water-diluted wort and pour it into a sterilized hydrometer tube (or use a refractometer). Record your initial gravity and temperature before adding the yeast. The target initial gravity is 1.072. If higher than that, dilute the wort with a little more water.

P. PITCH YOUR YEAST.

Use your thermometer to make sure the wort's temperature is between 65°F and 72°F (18°C and 22°C)—the ideal temperature for fermenting most ales in a 5-gallon (19 L) batch. The yeast will most likely come from a vial or slap pack, and most homebrew yeast packs are already premeasured for this size batch. Be very mindful of sanitation during this step; if the yeast comes in contact with a speck of food or dirt at this point, it can quickly become tainted. If you were brewing a lager batch, the process would be similar, but the target yeast pitching and fermenting temperature would be 15°F and 20°F (-9° and -7°C) cooler.

Q. ROCK THE BABY.

"Rock the baby" (or aerate) means to grab the top of the fermenter, lift it off-center, and twirl it back and forth. This will help to mix the yeast and air into the wort to ensure a good start to the fermentation process. Always exercise extreme caution when rocking a glass carboy.

R. SEAL THE TOP OF THE CARBOY WITH A STERILIZED RUBBER STOPPER AND AIRLOCK FILLED WITH STERILE WATER.

Check the wort each day. If you are having a strong, successful fermentation, you will have CO_2 bubbling through the airlock within 24 to 48 hours of pitching the yeast. You will also see a whitish, foamy yeast head forming on the top of your fermenting beer.

Read the hydrometer by bobbing it in a cylinder of beer.

S. LET THE BEER FERMENT.

At this point, you can start calling it beer, and as a new brewer, the first few days of that initial ferment can be fascinating. At this point, try to avoid opening the fermenter, as it is extremely vulnerable to bacteria and airborne yeasts. Try to keep the temperature of the beer between 68°F and 72°F (20°C and 22°C); that can be challenging because the fermentation itself creates heat. Wet towels can help wick away heat if needed. Depending on how much sugars you started with and what temperatures your are able to keep it at, most ferments on ales are extremely active for a few days and then start settling down after a week or so. Some higher-gravity beers and low temperature ferments can take much longer. Ideally, on most ales, you will let it ferment a minimum of ten days, even if it looks like it was done in three, so that yeast can absorb any off flavors and finish fermenting. You want the byproducts and yeast (called trub) to settle at the bottom and be left behind.

T. CHECK THE FINAL GRAVITY.

After a week or so, once the airlock has stopped bubbling for a few days and the beer looks a lot clearer, take another gravity reading with the hydrometer. The target final gravity is 1.010.

U. SIPHON THE BEER FOR BOTTLING.

After the fermentation is complete, siphon the beer into the sterilized bottling bucket. As you do this, add the corn sugar in 1 cup (235 ml) of boiling water. Stir until completely dissolved and then shut off your heat source.

V. ADD THE SUGAR WATER TO THE BOTTLING BUCKET AND GENTLY STIR WITH A SANITIZED STIRRING SPOON.

The sugar water is heavier than the beer you've added it to, so you are stirring to make sure that it thoroughly dilutes into the beer. This final sugar addition will be your source of carbonation in the bottle. Remember, when yeast eats sugar and converts it to alcohol, the natural byproduct is CO_2. By introducing more sugar to the beer just before bottling, you will allow the beer to re-ferment in the bottle. Since the CO_2 has nowhere to escape to, as it did through the airlock on top of the carboy, it goes into the solution and naturally carbonates your beer. Isn't Mother Nature awesome?

W. SANITIZE THE BOTTLES.

Sterilize your bottles using one of the sanitizing solutions. 22 ounce (650 ml) bottles or 25-ounce (750 ml) Champagne bottles are ideal to use for homebrewing, as they are much bigger than the standard 12-ounce (355 ml) beer bottle, allowing you to package a batch of beer in half the amount of time. The recipe yields roughly two cases of beer, but have a few extra bottles clean and handy, as you never know when one might break or get dirty.

Homebrewers enjoying the fruit of their labors.

X. BOTTLE THE BEER.

Fill the bottles until the liquid content is halfway up the thin part of the neck and then cap with sterilized bottle caps. Once your bottles are filled and capped, find a safe, 70°F (21°C) space in which to store them.

Y. STORE THE BOTTLED BEER BEFORE DRINKING.

Your bottled beer will need to be stored at room temperature (70–72°F [21–22°C]) for a couple weeks to give the yeast a chance to re-ferment and carbonate the bottles. After two weeks, throw a few bottles in the fridge for your next party and put the remaining bottles in a cool, dark place for aging. Since this beer has a targeted alcohol content of 9 percent by volume, it will age well. Be sure to date and label the bottles if you plan to have multiple batches of homebrew in your inventory at any given time.

Z. POP THE TOP ON A BOTTLE OF YOUR HOMEMADE BEER AND SHARE IT WITH A FRIEND.

Congrats, you've just completed your first batch of beer!

PART 2
EXTREME BREWING AT HOME

CHAPTER 1 DOGFISH HEAD RECIPES

CONTRIBUTED BY DOGFISH HEAD
LEAD BREWER BILL MARCHI

Ever since its humble beginnings at the Rehoboth, Delaware, brewpub in 1995, Dogfish Head has been known in craft beer circles for bucking antiquated brewing traditions, incorporating unique ingredients, and stretching the boundaries of beer styles.

If you're one of the lucky few that have worked between these walls, then you know that the commonality across all Dogfish Head coworkers is that we are a creative bunch and at times, even a little, well, off-centered. When you work at a place that has Ralph Waldo Emerson quotes inscribed across its walls, a giant metal steampunk treehouse in the front courtyard, and a whimsical peeing statue in the brewhouse (seriously, this is a real thing), it's not difficult to understand how the culture can drive creativity in our beers.

There's a certain depth to our beer that makes it unique to us: a merger of people, ideas, and passions all in a pint glass. At Dogfish Head, creative brewing is about making beers with a purpose and a story, often just as much about the journey as it is the destination. If you pull on the string of Dogfish beers, you will find a common thread throughout of music, literature, history, and culinary arts. These are the things that have great influence on us, so in turn, have great influence on our beer and what makes them so unique and creative—Beers like Midas Touch, Bitches Brew, Noble Rot, American Beauty, Chocolate Lobster, Theobroma, and Sixty-One to name a few. Something as simple as a jar of Sanka inspired the 2015 coworker small batch winning beer Mr. Hector Vargas, an imperial coffee porter (recipe on page 66) that was a nod to the 1980s cult classic film *Fast Times at Ridgemont High*. Or a challenge from our friends at *Pallet* magazine and an eloquently written passage from Shakespeare's Romeo and Juliet that were the basis for a bready Saison brewed with dates called Twenty Cunning Cooks (recipe on page 62).

It's pretty evident that inspiration at Dogfish Head comes from many places and people but is always directed to the pursuit and exploration of goodness in all that we do and especially in the creation of unique beers that can be enjoyed with our friends and loved ones.

20 CUNNING COOKS
FRUITED SAISON

Lady Capulet: "Hold, take these keys, and fetch more spices, Nurse."
Nurse: "They call for dates and quinces in the pastry."
Romeo and Juliet Act 4, Scene 4

With a little inspiration from our friends at *Pallet* magazine and a passage from Romeo and Juliet, we bring you 20 Cunning Cooks, a literary brew sure to make the Bard right proud! This saison was brewed with quinces and dates to provide a tart counterbalance to the doughy Maris Otter malt and flaked oats used in its mash bill. A Belgian ale yeast strain adds spicy notes and Jarrylo and Calypso hops lend fruity hop aromas of apple and pear.

Specific Recipe Information

Start with a preboil volume of 5.8 gallons. At flame out (after boil), carefully take about a liter of wort from your kettle and dissolve the date paste and quince paste in it, then add the mixture back to the kettle and start the whirlpool. Collect about 5 gallons of cooled wort in your fermenter or carboy. Ferment until gravity has stopped moving, approximately one week, and then transfer to a secondary vessel and let condition cold for another 2–3 weeks before bottling.

For All Grain: Heat your strike water up several degrees above the desired mash rest temperature. Single infusion mash with approximately 3.5 gallons of strike water. Vorlauf for about 10 minutes until your runoff clears. Sparge with approximately 3 gallons of 170°F water and collect enough runoff to hit the target preboil volume. Recipe based on 70% lautering efficiency.

KIT: EXTRACT

Malt Extracts/Additions

7 pounds Pale Malt Extract

8 ounces Maltodextrin

Turn burner off before adding. Boil for 60 minutes.

Steeping Grain

2 pounds Wheat Malt

1 pound Flaked Oats

Use a grain bag. Add to water immediately. Remove steeping grain at 170°F.

Hops

1 ounce Jarrylo (14.4% AA)

Bittering Hops boiled for 60 minutes

1 ounce Calypso (14.3% AA)

Aroma Hops added at whirlpool

Wort Clarifying Treatment

Whirlfloc (use ½ to 1 Tablet) – Add at last 5 minutes of the boil.

Yeast

3711 – Wyeast French Saison Ale or WLP590 – White Labs French Saison Ale.

Bottling

4 ounces Corn Sugar – Boil with 2 cups of water for 5 minutes.

KIT: ALL GRAIN

Grain / Mash Additions

5.5 pounds Maris Otter

2.5 pounds Wheat Malt

1 pound Carapils

1 pound Flaked Oats

Mash rest at 152°F for 45 minutes.

Hops

1 ounce Jarrylo (14.4% AA) – Bittering Hops are boiled for 60 minutes.

1 ounce Calypso (14.3% AA) – Aroma Hops are added at whirlpool

Other Additions

2 ounces Pitted Date Paste

2 ounces Quince Paste

Add fruit pastes at whirlpool.

Wort Clarifying Treatment

Whirlfloc (Use 1/2– 1 Tablet) – Add at last 5 minutes of the boil.

Yeast

3711 - Wyeast French Saison Ale or WLP590 - White Labs French Saison Ale

Bottling

4 ounces Corn Sugar – Boil with 2 cups of water for 5 minutes.

Estimated MoreBeer! Ranges	Extract
Estimated original gravity (OG)	1.048
Estimated SRM	5
Estimated IBU's	42
Estimated alcohol ABV %	4.8%
Suggested fermentation temperature	72°F

PUDDIN` WINE
ENGLISH BARLEYWINE

Estimated MoreBeer! Ranges	Extract	All Grain
Estimated original gravity (OG)	1.083	1.082
Estimated SRM	16.2	14.8
Estimated IBU's	39.8	39.8
Estimated alcohol ABV %	8.5%	8.6%
Suggested fermentation temperature	68°F	68°F

2017 Extreme Beer Fest Collaboration. Based on Jason Alström's recipe for a traditional Christmas pudding, this English-style Barleywine was brewed with Maris Otter malt and a boatload of dark and dried fruits—black currants, sultanas, plums, cherries, and raisins—plus golden treacle and brown sugar to goose the ABV to 11.8% ABV. Fermented with a traditional English ale yeast, our version then spent four months in freshly dumped Terra d'Oro Zinfandel Port wine barrels. It might be a Puddin' Wine, but this is not a beer to be trifled with.

Specific Recipe Information

Start with a preboil volume of 5.8 gallons. Prior to brewing, rehydrate the dried fruit in warm water, drain off most of the water, and macerate in a blender or food processor to make a paste that can be added at flameout. Collect about 5 gallons of cooled wort in your fermenter or carboy. Ferment until gravity has stopped moving, approximately one week, and then transfer to a secondary vessel for another 4–6 months of warm aging before bottling. For the last 2 weeks of secondary, consider adding 1 ounce of red wine-soaked medium toast French Oak cubes to complement the dark fruits in this beer.

For All Grain: Heat your strike water up several degrees above the desired mash rest temperature. Single infusion mash with approximately 4.5 gallons of strike water. Vorlauf for about 10 minutes until your runoff clears. Sparge with approximately 2.5 gallons of 170 F water and collect enough runoff to hit the target preboil volume. Recipe based on 70% lautering efficiency.

KIT: EXTRACT

Malt Extracts/Additions

10 pounds Pale Malt Extract

8 ounces Brown Sugar

8 ounces Lyle's Golden Syrup

8 ounces Maltodextrin

Turn burner off before adding. Boil for 60 minutes.

Steeping Grain

1 pound Toasted Wheat Flakes

8 ounces Special B Malt

2 ounces Hazelnut Flour

Use a grain bag. Add to water immediately. Remove steeping grain at 170°F.

Hops

1 ounce Warrior (16.8% AA) – Bittering Hops are boiled for 60 minutes.

1 ounce Kent Goldings (6.6% AA) – Aroma Hops are added at whirlpool.

Other Additions

8 ounces Dried Sultanas

8 ounces Dried Cherries

8 ounces Dried Black Currants

6 ounces Plum Juice Concentrate

4 ounces Raisin Juice Concentrate

2 ounces Black Currant Concentrate

1 teaspoon All-Spice

Add spices, fruit, and concentrates at whirlpool.

t last 5 minutes of the boil.

Yeast

1187 – Wyeast Ringwood Ale Yeast or WLP005 – White Labs British Ale Yeast

Bottling

4 ounces Corn Sugar – Boil with 2 cups of water for 5 minutes.

KIT: ALL GRAIN

Grain

8.25 pounds 2-Row Pilsner

4 pounds Maris Otter

1 pound Carapils

1 pound Flaked Wheat

8 ounces Special B Malt

8 ounces Brown Sugar

8 ounces Lyle's Golden Syrup

2 ounces Hazelnut Flour

Mash rest at 156°F for 30 minutes

Hops

1 ounce Warrior (16.8% AA) – Bittering Hops are boiled for 60 minutes.

1 ounce Kent Goldings (6.6% AA) – Aroma Hops are added at whirlpool.

Other Additions

8 ounces Dried Sultanas

8 ounces Dried Cherries

8 ounces Dried Black Currants

6 ounces Plum Juice Concentrate

4 ounces Raisin Juice Concentrate

2 ounces Black Currant Concentrate

1 teaspoon All-Spice

Add spices, fruit, and concentrates at whirlpool.

Wort Clarifying Treatment

Whirlfloc (use ½ to 1 Tablet) – Add at last 5 minutes of the boil.

Yeast

1187 – Wyeast Ringwood Ale Yeast or WLP005 – White Labs British Ale Yeast

Bottling

4 ounces Corn Sugar – Boil with 2 cups of water for 5 minutes.

DIRTY FERMENTINI
MARTINI INSPIRED
BLONDE ALE

2012 Extreme Beer Fest Collaboration. Inspired by a dirty martini, with olives as a funky and off-centered ingredient, which to our knowledge has never been used in a beer before. Along with the olives, we added the botanicals featured in Dogfish Head's small-batch distilled gin (whole leaf Cascade hops, juniper, black peppercorn, coriander, orange peel, lemon peel, and angelica root) to a Blonde Ale base that was then fermented dry with an ale yeast originating from a well-known London brewery (a nod to the popularity of gin in England). Just 5% ABV.

Specific Recipe Information

Start with a preboil volume of 5.7 gallons. Crush the juniper berry, peppercorn, and coriander prior to use. Dried orange peel and lemon peel can be replaced with the fresh peel from one medium-sized orange and one medium-sized lemon, respectively. Make sure you are using just the colored flesh of the peel and not the white pith as it will add an undesirable bitterness. Olive juice can be strained from your favorite jar of green olives (cured with water and salt) or be purchased as its own product. Depending on how dirty you like your martinis, you can add as much or as little olive juice as you'd like. Collect about 5 gallons of cooled wort in your fermenter or carboy. Ferment until gravity has stopped moving, approximately one week, and then transfer to a secondary vessel and let condition cold for another 2–3 weeks before bottling.

KIT: EXTRACT

Malt Extracts/Additions:

8 pounds Pale Malt Extract

12 ounces Maltodextrin

Turn burner off before adding. Boil for 60 minutes.

Hops

0.5 ounces Cascade (8.3% AA) – Bittering Hops are boiled for 60 minutes.

Other Additions

0.5 ounces Juniper Berry is boiled for 30 minutes.

0.5 ounces Peppercorn is boiled for 30 minutes.

0.25 ounces Coriander is boiled for 15 minutes.

0.25 ounces Angelica Root is boiled for 15 minutes.

0.125 ounces Dried Bitter Orange Peel is boiled for 15 minutes.

0.125 ounces Dried Lemon Peel is boiled for 15 minutes.

4 ounces Green Olive Juice is added at whirlpool.

Spices and citrus peels can be put in strainer bags for easy removal from the kettle.

Wort Clarifying Treatment

Whirlfloc (use ½ to 1 Tablet) – Add at last 5 minutes of the boil.

Yeast

1028 – Wyeast London Ale or WLP013 – White Labs London Ale

Bottling

4 ounces Corn Sugar – Boil with 2 cups of water for 5 minutes.

Estimated MoreBeer! Ranges	Extract
Estimated original gravity (OG)	1.048
Estimated SRM	7.3
Estimated IBU's	7.5
Estimated alcohol ABV %	4.2%
Suggested fermentation temperature	68°F

Beer Name

HE WHO SPELT IT
SPELT ALE

Spelt is an ancient staple grain from the Bronze Age and has many of the flavor characteristics of wheat. We decided to play on the nutty and spicy notes of the spelt with a big citrus blast of grapefruit peels and Citra hops from the Pacific Northwest.

Estimated MoreBeer! Ranges	Extract	All Grain
Estimated original gravity (OG)	1.050	1.053
Estimated SRM	7.8	6.5
Estimated IBU's	29.6	29.6
Estimated alcohol ABV %	4.8%	4.8%
Suggested fermentation temperature	72°F	72°F

Specific Recipe Information

Start with a preboil volume of 5.7 gallons. For the extract version of this recipe we're substituting spelt with wheat malt extract since spelt malt is not currently offered as an extract. If that ever changes, just substitute with the wheat malt extract at equal amounts. The dried grapefruit peel can be replaced with the fresh peel from 4 medium-sized grapefruits. Collect about 5 gallons of cooled wort in your fermenter or carboy. Ferment until gravity has stopped moving, approximately one week, and then transfer to a secondary vessel and let condition cold for another 2–3 weeks before bottling.

For All Grain: Heat your strike water up several degrees above the desired mash rest temperature. Single infusion mash with approximately 3.5 gallons of strike water. Vorlauf for about 10 minutes until your runoff clears. Sparge with approximately 3.0 gallons of 170 F water and collect enough runoff to hit the target preboil volume. Recipe based on 70% lautering efficiency.

KIT: EXTRACT

Malt Extracts/Additions

9 pounds Wheat Malt Extract

Turn burner off before adding. Boil for 60 minutes.

Hops

0.5 ounces Warrior (16.8% AA) – Bittering Hops are boiled for 60 minutes.

0.5 ounces Palisades (8.3% AA) – Flavor/Aroma Hops are added for 10 minutes.

0.5 ounces Citra (11.4% AA) – Aroma Hops are added at whirlpool.

Other Additions

1 ounce Dried Grapefruit Peel is added at whirlpool.

Wort Clarifying Treatment

Whirlfloc (use ½ to 1 Tablet) – Add at last 5 minutes of the boil.

Yeast

WLP566 – White Labs Belgian Saison II Ale

Bottling

4 ounces Corn Sugar – Boil with 2 cups of water for 5 minutes.

KIT: ALL GRAIN

Grain

5 pounds 2-Row Pilsner

5 pounds Malted Spelt

Mash rest at 153°F for 45 minutes.

Hops

0.5 ounces Warrior (16.8% AA) – Bittering Hops are boiled for 60 minutes.

0.5 ounces Palisades (8.3% AA) – Flavor/Aroma Hops are added for 10 minutes.

0.5 ounces Citra (11.4% AA) – Aroma Hops are added at whirlpool.

Other Additions

1 ounce Dried Grapefruit Peel is added at whirlpool.

Wort Clarifying Treatment

Whirlfloc (use ½ to 1 Tablet) – Add at last 5 minutes of the boil.

Yeast

WLP566 - White Labs Belgian Saison II Ale

Bottling

4 ounces Corn Sugar – Boil with 2 cups of water for 5 minutes.

MR. HECTOR VARGUS
IMPERIAL COFFEE PORTER

Mr. Hector Vargas was a Dogfish Head Coworker Small Batch winner and created by Dogfish coworkers Andrew Greeley, Grant Garrity, Matt Barthk, and Trey Bowden. This Imperial Coffee Porter is named after the pioneer Science teacher Mr. Hector Vargas from the 80's movie *Fast Times at Ridgemont High*. Mr. Hector Vargas ale is brewed with delicious Sanka decaf instant coffee...the same Sanka Mr. Vargas was drinking on the first day of school at Ridgemont High. This big porter has a ton of 2 row pale malt, some amber, caramel, wheat, black, and chocolate malts to accompany and complement the Sanka. We also added a touch of cinnamon and nutmeg to round it out. Everyone is in

Estimated MoreBeer! Ranges	Extract	All Grain
Estimated original gravity (OG)	1.091	1.090
Estimated SRM	35	34.5
Estimated IBU's	35.9	35.8
Estimated alcohol ABV %	8.4%	8.7%
Suggested fermentation temperature	68°F	68°F

Specific Recipe Information

Start with a preboil volume of 5.7 gallons. Collect about 5 gallons of cooled wort in your fermenter or carboy. Ferment until gravity has stopped moving, approximately one week, and then transfer to a secondary vessel and let condition cold for another 3-4 weeks before bottling.

For All Grain: Heat your strike water up several degrees above the desired mash rest temperature. Single infusion mash with approximately 6 gallons of strike water. Vorlauf for about 10 minutes until your runoff clears. Sparge with approximately 1.5 gallons of 170°F water and collect enough runoff to hit the target preboil volume. Recipe based on 70% lautering efficiency.

KIT: EXTRACT

Malt Extracts/Additions

14 pounds Pale Malt Extract

Turn burner off before adding. Boil for 60 minutes.

Steeping Grain

1 pound Amber Malt

1 pound Caramel Malt

8 ounces Wheat Malt

8 ounces Chocolate Malt

8 ounces Black (Patent) Malt

Use a grain bag. Add to water immediately. Remove steeping grain at 170°F.

Hops

1 ounce Warrior (16.8% AA) – Bittering Hops are boiled for 60 minutes.

1 ounce Amarillo (10.1% AA) – Aroma Hops are added for last 1 minute of boil.

Other Additions

1 ounce Decaffeinated Sanka

0.25 teaspoons Ground Nutmeg

0.25 teaspoons Ground Cinnamon

Add spices and Sanka at whirlpool.

Wort Clarifying Treatment

Whirlfloc (use ½ to 1 Tablet) – Add at last 5 minutes of the boil.

Yeast

1084 – Wyeast Irish Ale or WLP004 – White Labs Irish Ale

Bottling

4 ounces Corn Sugar – Boil with 2 cups of water for 5 minutes.

KIT: ALL GRAIN

Grain

15 pounds Pale 2-Row

2.25 pounds Amber Malt

1.5 pounds Caramel Malt

8 ounces Wheat Malt

8 ounces Black Patent

8 ounces Chocolate

Mash rest at 155°F for 30 minutes.

Hops

1 ounce Warrior (16.8% AA) – Bittering Hops are boiled for 60 minutes

1 ounce Amarillo (10.1% AA) – Aroma Hops are added for last 1 minute of boil.

Other Additions

1 ounce Decaffeinated Sanka

0.25 teaspoons Ground Nutmeg

0.25 teaspoons Ground Cinnamon

Wort Clarifying Treatment

Whirlfloc (use ½ to 1 Tablet) – Add at last 5 minutes of the boil.

Yeast

1084 – Wyeast Irish Ale or WLP004 – White Labs Irish Ale

Bottling

4 ounces Corn Sugar – Boil with 2 cups of water for 5 minutes.

PUNCH YOU IN THE RYE
BLACK RYE IPA

This beer was created and brewed by Dogfish Head coworkers Dan Weber, Ryan Mazur, and Ryan Yerdon for the Dogfish Head Coworker Small Batch competition. It is brewed with a blend of rye and chocolate malts that give the beer its spicy character and dark color. Strong citrus, fruity, and floral aromas are created from a heaping blend of Centennial, Amarillo, and Citra dryhops. It took two Rye-an's to bring this highly drinkable rye IPA to life!

Estimated MoreBeer! Ranges	Extract	All Grain
Estimated original gravity (OG)	1.069	1.068
Estimated SRM	27.4	26
Estimated IBU's	63.1	63
Estimated alcohol ABV %	6.6%	6.5%
Suggested fermentation temperature	68°F	68°F

Specific Recipe Information

Start with a preboil volume of 5.8 gallons. Collect about 5 gallons of cooled wort in your fermenter or carboy. Ferment until gravity has stopped moving, approximately one week, and then add the dry hops. After 4 days, transfer to a secondary vessel and let condition cold for another 2–3 weeks before bottling.

For All Grain: Heat your strike water up several degrees above the desired mash rest temperature and add the Gypsum. Single infusion mash with approximately 4.5 gallons of strike water. Vorlauf for about 10 minutes until your runoff clears. Sparge with approximately 2.5 gallons of 170°F water and collect enough runoff to hit the target preboil volume. Recipe based on 70% lautering efficiency.

KIT: EXTRACT

Malt Extracts/Additions

10.5 pounds Rye Malt Extract

Turn burner off before adding. Boil for 60 minutes.

Steeping Grain

2 pounds Caramel 80L

1 pound Chocolate Rye Malt

Use a grain bag. Add to water immediately. Remove steeping grain at 170°F.

Hops

1 ounce Warrior (16.8% AA) – Bittering Hops are boiled for 60 minutes.

1 ounce Centennial (10.3% AA) – Bittering/Flavor Hops are boiled for 30 minutes.

0.25 ounces Citra (11.4% AA) – Aroma Hops are added for last 1 minute of boil.

1 ounce Centennial (10.3% AA) – Dry Hop

1 ounce Amarillo (10.1% AA) – Dry Hop

0.5 ounce Citra (11.4% AA) – Dry Hop

Wort Clarifying Treatment

Whirlfloc (use ½ to 1 Tablet) – Add at last 5 minutes of the boil.

Yeast

1056 – Wyeast American Ale or WLP001 – White Labs California Ale

Bottling

4 ounces Corn Sugar – Boil with 2 cups of water for 5 minutes.

KIT: ALL GRAIN

Grain

8 pounds 2-Row Pilsner

2.1 pounds Crystal 80L

2 pounds Malted Rye

1.2 pounds Chocolate Rye

0.5 ounces Gypsum

Mash rest at 154°F for 30 minutes.

Hops

1 ounce Warrior (16.8% AA) – Bittering Hops are boiled for 60 minutes.

1 ounce Centennial (10.3% AA) – Bittering/Flavor Hops are boiled for 30 minutes.

0.25 ounces Citra (11.4% AA) – Aroma Hops are added for last 1 minute of boil.

1 ounce Centennial (10.3% AA) – Dry Hop

1 ounce Amarillo (10.1% AA) – Dry Hop

0.5 ounce Citra (11.4% AA) – Dry Hop

Wort Clarifying Treatment

Whirlfloc (use ½ to 1 Tablet) – Add at last 5 minutes of the boil.

Yeast

1056 – Wyeast American Ale or WLP001 – White Labs California Ale

Bottling

4 ounces Corn Sugar - Boil with 2 cups of water for 5 minutes.

SZESSION IPA
SESSION PEPPER IPA

Szession IPA brings a little heat to the party with this twist on a session IPA. Featuring a lower ABV and huge bursts of tropical and piney hoppiness from numerous additions of Topaz, Amarillo, and Simcoe, the brew finishes with a healthy dose of heat from Szechuan pepper added to the whirlpool.

Specific Recipe Information

Start with a preboil volume of 5.8 gallons. For maximum heat, crush or grind the Szechuan pepper in a spice grinder before adding it to the whirlpool. Collect about 5 gallons of cooled wort in your fermenter or carboy. Ferment until gravity has stopped moving, approximately one week, and then transfer to a secondary vessel and let condition cold for another 2-3 weeks before bottling.

KIT: EXTRACT

Malt Extracts/Additions:

7 pounds Pale Malt Extract

Turn burner off before adding. Boil for 60 minutes.

Steeping Grain

1.0 pound Caramel 60L

Use a grain bag. Add to water immediately. Remove steeping grain at 170°F.

Hops

1 ounce Topaz (16.5% AA) – Bittering Hops are boiled for 60 minutes.

1 ounce Topaz (16.5% AA) – Flavor/Aroma Hops are boiled for 10 minutes.

1 ounce Simcoe (10.3% AA) – Flavor/Aroma Hops are boiled for 10 minutes.

1 ounce Topaz (16.5% AA) – Aroma Hops are added for last 1 minute of boil.

1 ounce Simcoe (10.3% AA) – Aroma Hops are added for last 1 minute of boil.

1 ounce Amarillo (10.1% AA) – Aroma Hops are added for last 1 minute of boil.

Other Additions

0.2 ounces Szechuan Pepper

Add pepper at whirlpool.

Wort Clarifying Treatment

Whirlfloc (use ½ to 1 Tablet) – Add at last 5 minutes of the boil.

Yeast

1056 – Wyeast American Ale or WLP001 – White Labs California Ale

Bottling

4 ounces Corn Sugar – Boil with 2 cups of water for 5 minutes.

Estimated MoreBeer! Ranges	Extract
Estimated original gravity (OG)	1.048
Estimated SRM	71
Estimated IBU's	96.6
Estimated alcohol ABV %	4.6%
Suggested fermentation temperature	68°F

Beer Name

WRATH OF PECANT
BROWN-ISH ALE

2010 Extreme Beer Fest Collaboration. We brewed this 6% ABV brownish ale with smoked pecan-wood malt and four other malt varieties, plantain flour, and carob, a brown powder made from the seed pods of the carob tree that are rich in sugar and similar in taste to chocolate. It makes for a complex but quaffable beer with a malty and nutty character balanced by subtle earthy notes. The name, of course, is a tongue-in-cheek reference to the 1982 science fiction film Star Trek II: The Wrath of Khan and was chosen by BeerAdvocate members.

Estimated MoreBeer! Ranges	Extract	All Grain
Estimated original gravity (OG)	1.071	1.070
Estimated SRM	7.9	7
Estimated IBU's	43	43
Estimated alcohol ABV %	6%	6.6%
Suggested fermentation temperature	68°F	68°F

Specific Recipe Information

Start with a preboil volume of 5.8 gallons. You can opt to use commercially available smoked malt or, if you have a smoker or barbeque grill, you can try smoking your own pale or pilsner malt using pecan-wood or pecan-wood chips. Mash up the plantain before adding to expose the starches. Collect about 5 gallons of cooled wort in your fermenter or carboy. Ferment until gravity has stopped moving, approximately one week, and then transfer to a secondary vessel and let condition cold for another 2–3 weeks before bottling.

For All Grain: Heat your strike water up several degrees above the desired mash rest temperature and add the Gypsum. Single infusion mash with approximately 4.5 gallons of strike water. Vorlauf for about 10 minutes until your runoff clears. Sparge with approximately 2.5 gallons of 170 F water and collect enough runoff to hit the target preboil volume. Recipe based on 70% lautering efficiency.

KIT: EXTRACT

Malt Extracts/Additions

10.5 pounds Pilsner Malt Extract Turn burner off before adding. Boil for 60 minutes.

Steeping Grain

1.5 pounds Smoked Malt

1 pound Special Roast

1 pound Caramel 30L

1 medium sized Plantain

Use a grain bag. Add to water immediately. Remove steeping grain at 170°F.

Hops

1 ounce CTZ (16.2% AA) – Bittering Hops are boiled for 60 minutes.

1 ounce Willamette (4.7% AA) – Flavor Hops are boiled for 15 minutes

Other Additions

1.75 ounces Carob – Added for last 5 minutes of boil.

Wort Clarifying Treatment

Whirlfloc (use ½ to 1 Tablet) – Add at last 5 minutes of the boil.

Yeast

1187 – Wyeast Ringwood Ale Yeast or WLP005 – White Labs British Ale Yeast

Bottling

4 ounces Corn Sugar – Boil with 2 cups of water for 5 minutes.

KIT: ALL GRAIN

Grain

9.5 pounds 2-Row Pilsner Malt

1.5 pounds Smoked Malt

1 pound Caramel 30L

8 ounces Extra Special Roast

0.5 ounces Gypsum

1 medium sized Plantain

Mash rest at 155°F for 30 minutes.

Hops

1 ounce CTZ (16.2% AA) – Bittering Hops are boiled for 60 minutes.

1 ounce Willamette (4.7% AA) – Flavor Hops are boiled for 15 minutes.

Wort Clarifying Treatment

Whirlfloc (use ½ to 1 Tablet) – Add at last 5 minutes of the boil.

Yeast

1187 – Wyeast Ringwood Ale Yeast or WLP005 – White Labs British Ale Yeast

Bottling

4 ounces Corn Sugar – Boil with 2 cups of water for 5 minutes.

CHAPTER 2 CONTRIBUTED RECIPES

7VENTH SUN BREWERY

DUNEDIN, FLORIDA

Beer Name

OR IT GETS THE GOSE AGAIN

Founded in Dunedin, Florida, by Devon Kreps and Justin Stange, 7venth Sun held its grand opening on January 7, 2012. The partners met at Sweetwater Brewing in Atlanta where Stange worked in brewing, cellar, and packaging operations and Kreps was production manager. Prior to Sweetwater, Kreps had graduated from Oregon State University with a degree in fermentation science, brewed at Anheuser-Busch's pilot facility, and held a manager position at AB's Cartersville, Georgia, location. Meanwhile, Stange, after moving to Tampa Bay to start 7venth Sun, first ended up as one of Cigar City Brewing's earliest employees. Although the 7venth Sun team originally intended to open a large production facility in Tampa, the housing bubble burst, leaving them struggling to find funding. Taking a step back, they instead decided to open a smaller facility in the coastal town of Dunedin, about twenty-five miles west of Tampa. Ultimately though, starting small proved serendipitous as it allowed the brewery to release a wide variety of beer styles, which ended up being an extremely liberating departure from the setting at a large production brewery.

While working out new recipes for their young brewery, Florida Weisse, a fruity twist on the tart German Berliner Weisse, stepped onto the scene. Inspired by Professor Fritz Briem's 1809 Berliner Weisse, the pair thought it was a perfect style to complement Florida's sunshine and warmer temperatures. Collaborating with some of the area's other burgeoning breweries, they discussed process ideas and dipped into the vast availability of tropical and citrus fruits the state had to offer. Beers like Dancin' in the Streets (made with watermelon), Do you Even Sudachi, Bro? (made with sudachi, a Japanese citrus fruit), and Key Lime Sublime were the result. It was the beginning of a path that set the tone for 7venth Sun—innovating and reinterpreting traditional styles by taking a new approach. Since then, 7venth Sun has continued to push the limits of style descriptions and categories, shifting somewhat to focus on barrel-aged beer, both sour and spirit-aged, wild fermentation, and creative takes on Saisons and IPAs.

The Gose originates from central Germany and is typically associated with Leipzig, the largest city in the German State of Saxony. Like Berliner Weisse, it's tart, refreshing, and low in alcohol. It was traditionally spiced with coriander, however, in 7th Sun's twist on the original, the cucumbers balance with the salinity and tartness of this beer style, making it a refreshing option in hot weather in spite of its savory foundation. When it came time to name it, the brewery decided on "Or It Gets the Gose Again," a reference to the 1991 film *The Silence of the Lambs*. Quid pro quo, Clarice.

	Extract	All Grain
Estimated original gravity (OG)	1.030–1.040	1.030–1.040
Estimated SRM	2–3	2–3
Estimated IBU's	10–15	7–10
Estimated alcohol ABV %	4.5%	4.5%
Suggested fermentation temperature	68°F	68°F

Specific Recipe Information

Boil for 15 minutes and reduce temperature to 110°F and pitch Wyeast 5335 Lactobacillus. If possible, bubble the wort with CO_2. Purge the kettle headspace with CO_2 and cover. Allow the wort to rest for 24 to 72 hours—continuing to purge the kettle headspace with CO_2 when possible (every 9 hours minimum). After resting, boil for 45 minutes, add hops, and 5 minutes before end of the boil add 0.70 ounces of sea salt. When fermentation is complete, add 3 pounds peeled and sliced cucumber in a nylon bag for 24 to 48 hours.

KIT: EXTRACT

Malt Extracts/Additions
5 pounds Wheat DME

Turn burner off before adding. Boil for 60 minutes.

Steeping Grain
None

Hops
0.55 ounces Hallertau Mittelfruh at start of the boil (45 minutes).

Wort Clarifying Treatment
Whirlfloc (use ½ to 1 Tablet) —add at last 5 minutes of the boil.

KIT: ALL GRAIN

Grain
6 pounds Pilsner

3 pounds German Wheat

2.5 ounces Acidulated Malt

Turn burner off before adding. Boil for 60 minutes.

Recipe based on:
70% Mash Efficiency

Strike Water Temperature:
164°F

Mash Temperature:
147°F

Time:
30 minutes

Sparge Water Temperature:
170°F

Time:
2 hours depending on lauter

Hop
0.55 ounces Hallertau Mittelfruh at start of the boil (45 minutes).

Wort Clarifying Treatment
Whirlfloc (use ½ to 1 Tablet) – Add at last 5 minutes of the boil.

AGAINST THE GRAIN BREWERY & SMOKEHOUSE

LOUISVILLE KENTUCKY

Beer Name

OLD IPALE

Louisville's only brewer-owned brewery is, like most worthwhile undertakings, the product of dissatisfaction with the status quo. The Louisville area has had a number of quality brewpubs for some time now, but still, there simply was not enough beer in Kentucky's largest city. Against the Grain is an effort to help solve this problem. Partners Jerry Gnagy, Sam Cruz, Adam Watson, and Andrew Ott opened their brewpub in October 2011 at the intersection of Jackson and Main Street in the corner of Louisville Slugger Field. They maintain a diverse array of beers covering all of the major categories of beer flavor (hop, smoke, dark, malt, and session) while generating an endless stream of innovative new brews. Fan favorites include Against the Grain's hop-forward Double IPA Citra Ass Down; Mac FannyBaw, a barrel-aged Rauchbier inspired by Islay Scotch Whisky; and Bloody Show, a blood orange Pilsner made in collaboration with Mikkeller. In short, everything is "specialty." At this brewery and smokehouse, boredom will be extremely difficult to find. In 2015, a new brewery, warehouse, tasting room, and retail space was added to meet rising demand for Against the Grain beers.

The food is designed with the same philosophy the partners follow in their brewing. Fresh and interesting smokehouse fare with a gastropub flare lets Against the Grain bring its guests the very best flavors to both stand alone and complement a rotating selection of beers. Smoked, cured, dry-rubbed, and grilled is the name of the game. What's that? You want something sweet? How about donut holes with raspberry jam and custard made from our 35K Milk Stout. Regular menu changes allow the brewpub to take full advantage of the best seasonal ingredients, the whims of its chef, and the optimal pairings its dynamic beer list offers. Throw your preconceived notions right the hell out of the window. This isn't just another brewpub.

This is another beer from Against the Grain Brewery that's meant to mess with your minds as well as your taste buds. What's so old about old ales? Historically, these were stronger beers that spent many months in wooden casks or barrels, but most old ales produced today are not in fact that old and aren't even that interesting. So Against the Grain decided to make an old ale that takes ingredients old folks love and put them in something the brewery's four founders wanted to drink. This IPA is balanced and super fruity with additions of prune juice, elderflower, and Lemondrop hops. It will keep you dancing the Charleston like it's 1920 again. Coo coo ca-choo, Mrs. Robinson.

	Extract	All Grain
Estimated original gravity (OG)	1.067	None Provided
Estimated SRM	6.4	
Estimated IBU's	68	
Estimated alcohol ABV %	7.9%	
Suggested fermentation temperature	67°F	

KIT: EXTRACT

Specific Recipe Information

Mash all grain at 153°F for 60 minutes. Boil for 60 minutes. adding hops at specified intervals. Add elderflower at flame out. Add prune juice to cooled wort in fermenter and pitch healthy ale yeast. Dry hop after primary fermentation with 1 ounce Citra and 0.5 ounces Mosaic for 4 days. Rack, prime, or force carb as normal.

Malt Extracts/Additions

8 pounds Light Liquid Malt Extract

2 pounds Liquid Wheat Malt Extract

Turn burner off before adding. Boil for 60 minutes.

Steeping Grain

None

Hops

1 ounce Bravo (15.5%AA) at 60 minutes.

0.5 ounce Chinook (13%AA) at 20 minutes.

1 ounce Lemondrop (6%AA) at 5 minutes.

1 ounce Citra (14.5%AA) at 5 minutes.

Wort Clarifying Treatment

Whirlfloc (use ½ to 1 Tablet) – Add at last 5 minutes of the boil.

KIT: ALL GRAIN

Grain

8 pounds Pale Ale

1 pound Munich 10

1 pound White Wheat malt

1 pound Golden Naked Oats

32 ounces prune juice

1 ounce Elderflower

Recipe based on: 70% Mash Efficiency

Strike Water Temperature: N/A

Mash Temperature: 153°F

Time: 60 minutes

Sparge Water Temperature: 168°F

Time: N/A

Hops

1 ounce Bravo (15.5%AA) at 60 minutes.

0.5 ounce Chinook (13%AA) at 20 minutes.

1 ounce Lemondrop (6%AA) at 5 minutes.

1 ounce Citra (14.5%AA) at 5 minutes.

Wort Clarifying Treatment

Whirlfloc (use ½ to 1 Tablet) – Add at last 5 minutes of the boil.

ALLAGASH BREWING COMPANY

PORTLAND MAINE

ALLAGASH AVANCE

AMERICAN WILD ALE

Founded in Portland, Maine, in 1995, Allagash Brewing Company is dedicated to crafting the best Belgian-inspired beers in the world. Best known for its flagship beer, Allagash White, the brewery has also gained notability for brewing wild, sour, and spontaneously fermented beers with the help of age-old Belgian methods. Founder Rob Tod has a story of the early days of Allagash, in which he bought glasses of Allagash White for bar patrons around Maine, only to have them point to the cloudy beer and ask, "What's wrong with it?" Drinkers today understand this golden, hazy color as a signature of Belgian-style wheat beers. Since pouring its first glass, Allagash has sought to expand American palates by introducing them to Belgian brewing traditions.

Allagash continued to push itself and its audience's taste buds by becoming one of the early adopters of barrel aging and 100 percent bottle conditioning. In 2004, Allagash launched Curieux, a Belgian Tripel aged for up to eight weeks in bourbon barrels. The same year, brewmaster Jason Perkins found an unexpected, wild strain of yeast in one of his batches. Instead of chucking

the batch, he and Tod chose to cultivate it. Luckily for Allagash, this native organism turned out to be a unique, Maine-only strain of *Brettanomyces*, a type of yeast now used in beers like Little Brett, Confluence, and Interlude. Pushing their microflora game a step further and looking to the future, employees on a five-day canoe trip down the Allagash River took samples of microorganisms native to the river's air, which are also now being cultivated in the lab.

In 2007, Allagash built a coolship and became one of the first U.S. breweries to experiment with spontaneous fermentation. The coolship, a shallow, rectangular, room-sized pan, is traditionally used in the creation of Belgian Lambics. After brewing, cooling wort spends an entire night in the coolship, exposed to the elements. During that time, naturally occurring microflora inoculate the beer, which is then transferred to French oak wine barrels where the fermentation takes anywhere from one to three years. These spontaneously fermented beers—like Coolship Cerise, an ale aged on fresh Maine cherries—emerge with mild tartness and complex flavor.

Avancé is a complex, sour ale with aromas of strawberry preserves and toasted oak. Berries and an additional touch of oak continue in the flavor, which concludes with a warm, sweet finish. The beer is brewed with multiple sugars including molasses, date sugar, white cane sugar, and dark rock candi. It's then fermented with three different yeast strains and aged in oak bourbon barrels for a year with *Lactobacillus* and *Pediococcus*. After transferring the beer to stainless, we add one-pound-per-gallon of fresh, locally picked strawberries and age it for another six months. While Avancé (9.5% ABV) certainly isn't quick or simple to produce, we think the resulting beer is well worth the effort.

	Extract	All Grain
Estimated original gravity (OG)	1.088	
Estimated SRM	35	35
Estimated IBU's	35	85
Estimated alcohol ABV %	10.5%	10.5%
Suggested fermentation temperature	68°F	

Specific Recipe Information

Dissolve Malt extract in water. Steep grains in bag for 30 minutes at 150°F. Use Wyeast 3864 for primary and Wyeast 3463 for secondary fermentation. Age beer in bourbon barrel or with bourbon soaked oak spirals for 6 months with *Lacotbacillis* cultures. After souring is complete, age beer on 7.5 pounds of freshly picked strawberries for six additional months.

KIT: EXTRACT

Malt Extracts/Additions

8.5 pounds Amber Malt Extract

4.8 ounces sucrose

3.2 ounces dark candi syrup

2.4 ounces molasses

2 ounces date sugar

Steeping Grain

2 pounds Munich 10 L

9.5 ounces Caramel 120 L

Use a grain bag. Add to water immediately. Remove steeping grain at 170°F.

Hops

0.5 ounces Perle

0.75 ounces Hallertauer Mittelfrueh

0.5 ounces Tettnang

0.5 ounces Czech Saaz

Bittering Hops boiled for 90 minutes.

Bittering Hops are boiled for 45 minutes.

Bittering/Flavor Hops are boiled for 15 minutes.

Aroma Hops are added at whirlpool

Wort Clarifying Treatment

KICK Carageenan (1 Tablet) – Add at last 5 minutes of the boil.

Bottling

4 ounces Corn Sugar –boil with 2 cups of water for 5 minutes.

KIT: ALL GRAIN

Target Original Extract: 21 Plato

Target SRM: 35

Target IBU: 35

Target ABV: 10.5%

Grain

70% Pilsner Malt

15% Munich 10 L

5% Caramel 120 L

2% Carapils

1.5% date sugar

Mash Temp: 150°F. Hold for 45 minutes.

Sugar

1% molasses

2% dark candi syrup

2.5% granulated sucrose

Hops

90 minute boil

Hop 1 (at boil): Perle

Hop 2 (boil + 45 minutes): Hallertau Mittlfrueh

Hop 3 (boil + 75 minutes): Tettnang

Hop 4 (whirlpool/flame out): Czech Saaz

Yeasts

Primary Fermentation: Wyeast 3864 at 68°F

Secondary Fermentation: Wyeast 3463 at 70°F

Also add 1% boiled Granulated Sugar

Post Fermentation Process

Age beer in a bourbon barrel or with bourbon-soaked oak spirals for 6 months with *Lacotbacillis* cultures. After souring is complete, age beer on freshly picked strawberries (1.5 pounds per gallon) for 6 additional months.

BANDED HORN BREWING COMPANY

BIDDEFORD MAINE

Beer Name

LOST IN FERMENTATION
BARREL-AGED AMBER ALE

● ●

After spending five years as the head brewer of a well-known brewery in Brooklyn, Ian McConnell returned to his home state of Maine with the goal of opening a production brewery in Portland. His cousin Ron Graves, who had originally convinced McConnell to start brewing his own beer years earlier, jumped on board right away. Time spent scouring the real estate market in and around Portland led them to discover the Pepperell Mill in nearby Biddeford. Well into its own journey of revitalization, the pair decided that the old New England mill town was the perfect place for a brave new brewery to take root.

The mill complex and the city itself seemed to have chosen them, and from that point on, launching the company was a breeze. Today, Banded Horn focuses on brewing original beers in a wide array of styles with an intense focus on dry, sessionable ales and all kinds of lagers. Lacking a true flagship, the brand is nonetheless willing to stake its reputation on Pepperell Pilsener, a well-hopped, dry, and spicy German-style Pilsener. Already an avid explorer of lagers during his homebrewing years, Ian solidified his desire and ability to perfect these styles in an American setting after traveling around Europe and learning from German brewmasters.

Banded Horn experiments with all kinds of ales and lagers and is always up for a new challenge. For Portland Beer Week in 2014, Shahin Khojastehzad of Novare Res Bier Cafe challenged Maine breweries to concoct Bill Murray-themed beers in an effort to entice the actor to show up and try some of them. Eager to participate, Banded Horn dreamed up Lost in Fermentation, modeling it after what Murray's character in the 2003 film *Lost in Translation* might have sought in a beer.

Lost in Fermentation is a strong, sexy, scarlet ale that's aged on Suntory Hibiki whisky-soaked oak chips and dry hopped with Simcoe and Azacca hops. Bill Murray may have lost his way in traffic during the movie, but Lost in Fermentation never veered from its delicious course–it was a huge success. Sadly, only five gallons (19 L) were made when this beer first debuted, and all of it disappeared before most of the Banded Horn crew got to the event, but it's sure to be repeated someday. In the meantime, why not make your own batch?

	Extract	All Grain
Estimated original gravity (OG)	1.074	None Provided
Estimated SRM	13.85	
Estimated IBU's	60	
Estimated alcohol ABV %	7.8%	
Suggested fermentation temperature	68°F	

Specific Recipe Information

Malts based on a 78% efficiency. Use a netural water profile with recommended minimal amounts of ions. Mash at 152°F for a balance of fermentability and mouthfeel. Use US-05 or similar clean/dry low ester, medium to high alcohol tolerance ale yeast. After fermentation is ceased for two days, transfer to secondary on top of dry hops and oak chips. Make sure the oak chips have soaked in just enough whiskey to cover them for about a week: 3 ounces is quite a bit, so you shouldn't need more than 3 to 4 days contact time. If you wish for more contact time, add the oak chips first and the dry hops 2 to 3 days before packaging. This beer will have a great shelf life, but for the best hop flavors and peak malt flavor, it will be best between 2 and 4 weeks after packaging. The whiskey/oak flavors will hold up very well, and it will change slowly over time into a sweeter, smoother profile.

KIT: EXTRACT

Malt Extracts/Additions

9.5 pounds Pale Liquid Extract

Turn burner off before adding. Boil for 60 minutes.

Steeping Grain

4 pounds Weyermann Carared

0.75 pounds Best Caramel Malt Pils (or similar Dextrin Malt)

Use a grain bag. Add to water immediately. Remove steeping grain at 170°F.

Hops

1 ounce Nugget (13% AA)—boil for 60 minutes.

1 ounce Nugget (13% AA)—boil for 10 minutes.

1 ounce Nugget (13% AA)—boil for at flame out

1 ounce Simcoe dry-hop

1 ounce Azacca dry-hop

Wort Clarifying Treatment

Whirlfloc (use ½ to 1 Tablet) – Add at last 5 minutes of the boil.

KIT: ALL GRAIN

Grain

13 pounds Rahr Standard 2-Row

4 pounds Weyermann Carared

0.75 pounds Best Malz Caramel Malt Pils

BARRELED SOULS BREWING COMPANY

SACO MAINE

Beer Name

COOKIE MONSTER
IMPERIAL PORTER

Chris Schofield and Matthew Mills, who have known each other since childhood, opened Barreled Souls Brewing Company on July 19, 2014, in Saco, Maine. After visiting breweries throughout the country and drinking far too many great beers together, the idea to open a brewery started to take shape. They decided early on that not only did they want to make a wide range of beers and truly embrace extreme beer culture, they wanted to physically make beer in a unique way. Several years back, while reading *Yeast* by Jamil Zainasheff and Chris White, Schofield came across the concept of a Burton Union system. The whole theory behind the system struck him as a great way to achieve healthy fermentations, add unique characteristics to the beer, and pull a healthy, almost selectively bred yeast crop from every batch.

Since no one in the world does this with 100 percent of their beers, some initial skepticism seemed more than warranted. In the end, Mills' background in the wine industry and general love of barrels ended up persuading him. With limited guidance, except for a few emails from Firestone Walker's Matt Brynildson, they designed and built the system. Producing 100 percent barrel-fermented beers and maintaining their clean Scottish house yeast strain, all while operating out of the basement of a 100-year-old home,

has certainly presented some challenges. But in Barreled Souls, Schofield and Mills have created the brewery they want to spend time at and the beers they want to drink.

There's a quote from Peter Bouckaert, head brewer at New Belgium, that Schofield has always liked: "Americans think it's great to be consistent; Belgians try to be consistently great." It's led the partners to the idea that consistency can be the enemy of experience. The beers they make again and again always have the same concept, but are never quite the same, and while Barreled Souls strives for excellence, it's never beholden to precision. Schofield and Mills liken their approach to a chef walking through a farmers market evaluating ingredients and developing ideas for what will become the next dish. The result will never be an exact replica of what was made before, but the customer will always get something beautiful and a genuinely special experience.

If asked to list their top ten favorite commercial beers, there's a good chance Chris and Matt would each list ten barrel-aged beers. Barrel aging in freshly emptied spirit barrels is a method of adding complexity and depth to beer. Melding the original beer with the characteristics of the spirit, the texture and flavor of the oak, and the slow oxidation of the wood creates a completely new and, hopefully, perfectly integrated product. To date, Barreled Souls has dedicated one-third of its production to a barrel-aging program.

Cookie Monster is a beer that Mills and Schofield developed after one of their assistant brewers, Jesse Painter, brought up the idea of brewing a beer made with 100 percent maple sap. Combining the wood and earth flavors of raw maple sap with the roasted and dark chocolate characteristics of an Imperial Porter seemed a natural fit. Plus, pairing walnuts and raisins with maple is a classic cookie combination.

Once the concept was developed, they had to decide how to achieve it through the brewing process. Using raw maple sap was pretty straightforward. The specific gravity of the sap is measured and added to the predicted gravity of the grain bill. Introducing raisin and walnut character is a bit more complicated since Barreled Souls insists on using real ingredients. Raisins contain significant amounts of sugar and need to be fermented, so they must be added prior to or during fermentation. To achieve this, Schofield and Mills made a puree and added it directly to the mash. The walnuts, on the other hand, derive most of their character from the volatile oils which will all but disappear in the boil or during fermentation. The solution is to submerge a mesh bag of walnuts in the conditioning tanks for five to seven days. The cold tank temperature along with the bag prevent the fat in the walnuts from becoming soluble in the beer and ruining mouth feel and head retention.

The resulting beer has the aroma of roasted walnuts with a hint of dark fruit from the raisins. The mouthfeel is full bodied and rich with earthy flavors from the maple sap.

	Extract	All Grain
Estimated original gravity (OG)	1.092–1.095	None Provided
Estimated SRM	48	
Estimated IBU's	46–50	
Estimated alcohol ABV %	9.6–10%	
Suggested fermentation temperature	63 to 65°F	

Specific Recipe Information

Heat your sap to your desired strike temperature in order to hit a mash temp of 156°F. Add 2 pounds of raisins to a container large enough to cover them with hot sap. Add enough sap so the raisins can double in size (they soak up a lot). Leave them for about an hour and then take an immersion blender to them and create a fine raisin-sap puree. Mix this puree into the mash once you added all the grain. Single infusion mash this for 60 minutes and Vorlauf for 10 minutes. Spare with 165°F sap until you've hit your target kettle volume—a 75 minute boil. Use Wyeast 1728 and ferment in low 60's. Transfer to secondary and add 2 pounds of crushed and toasted walnuts in a mesh bag for 5 to 7 days.

KIT: EXTRACT

Malt Extracts/Additions

12 pounds Light Dried Malt Extract

Steeping Grain

1 pound Chocolate Malt

12 ounces Special B Malt

12 ounces Crystal 45 L

12 ounces Black Patent Malt

2 pounds raisins

Hops

1.5 ounces Magnum

1 ounce Glacier

Bittering hops are added as first wort hops.

Bittering hops are boiled for 10 minutes.

Wort Clarifying Treatment

Whirlfloc (1 Tablet) – Add at last 5 minutes of the boil.

KIT: ALL GRAIN

Grain

15 pounds Maris Otter

5 pounds American 2-Row

1 pound Chocolate Malt

12 ounces Special B Malt

12 ounces Crystal 45 L

12 ounces Black Patent Malt

2 pounds raisins

Recipe based on 70% mash efficiency

Strike water temperature: 165°F

Mash temperature: 156°F

Time: 45 minutes

Sparge water temperature: 165°F

Time: 60 minutes

Hops

1.5 ounces Magnum

1 ounce Glacier

Bittering hops are added as first wort hops.

Bittering hops are boiled for 10 minutes.

BEAU'S ALL NATURAL BREWING COMPANY

VANKLEEK HILL ONTARIO

GRANDMASTER O.G.

IMPERIAL GRUIT

The plan to start up Beau's All Natural was conceived more than a decade ago, over pints on a sunny summer patio. A lifelong entrepreneur, Tim Beauchesne was looking for a new project—something fun this time, he had decided—and he asked his son Steve whether he might want to start a craft brewery. The idea sparked their imagination, so they set to work, and two years later, on July 1, 2006, the first glass of Beau's flagship Lug Tread Lagered Ale was poured.

Steve's do-it-yourself ethic, inspired by his time spent running an indie music label and promoting bands, became a driving force behind Beau's DIY approach to making beer. As the brewery quickly grew, Steve and Tim filled key roles with friends and family, creating a close-knit group of loyal employees, and building a fun, fiercely independent company culture, all the while running a brewery in a rural village with more cows than people.

Along the way, where other local breweries zigged, Beau's zagged, choosing to make certified organic beer, for example, and packaging it in four-packs instead of six-packs. When it came time to consider additional beers to complement the flagship brand, Beau's looked to Gruits and in particular, a locally available herb called bog myrtle. In 2008, Beau's created Bog

Water, its first Gruit ale. Beau's has since developed a Gruit Series with four annual releases timed to solstices and equinoxes and an experimental beer series it calls Wild Oats. Additionally, the brewery celebrates FeBREWary each year, releasing a new beer each week for the month. In total, Beau's releases more than fifty beers annually and is almost constantly working on some creative new beer project.

Beau's has been a recipient of more than eighty-five awards for brewing, packaging design, and business practices, including two Gold medals at Mondial de la Bière, six Gold medals at the Canadian Brewing Awards, seven wins as Best Craft Brewery in Ontario, and seven more as Best Regularly Produced Beer in Ontario at the Golden Tap Awards. In 2013, Beau's became Canada's first B-Corp brewery, a certification of higher standards of social and environmental performance, transparency, and accountability. And in July 2016, Beau's began the process of transferring ownership of the brewery to its employees, securing its future as a totally independent Canadian craft brewery.

Beau's approach to extreme brewing starts with collaboration. Managers from every department meet weekly to taste beer, discuss ideas, and solve challenges. Brewmaster Matthew O'Hara plays the role of conductor, tapping the talents his fellow employee-owners for inspiration.

Calculated risk-taking is also part of Beau's ethos. Beer concept ideas often take the team into unknown territory, but Beau's is willing to take a chance. Working with foragers and local farmers also allows access to new flavors and brewing ingredients.

Balance is the final tenant and lends equilibrium to the risk-taking. Beau's aims to create classy, complex, and approachable beer, rather than something so extreme it overwhelms or becomes one-dimensional.

	Extract	All Grain
Estimated original gravity (OG)	1.070–1.074	1.070–1.074
Estimated SRM	6	6
Estimated IBU's	15	15
Estimated alcohol ABV %	8%	8%
Suggested fermentation temperature	68°F	68°F

Specific Recipe Information

In Beau's Gruit Series, herbs and botanicals replace a dominant hop character. Grandmaster O.G. employs common ingredients to the style (Labrador tea, bog myrtle, and yarrow) in addition to thyme. The flavor is herbaceous, mildly sweet, and slightly peppery. It won Silver at the Canadian Brewing Awards in 2015.

KIT: EXTRACT

Malt Extracts/Additions

10.5 pounds Light Malt Extract

Turn burner off before adding. Boil for 90 minutes.

Steeping Grain

1 pound Munich

Use a grain bag. Add to water immediately. Remove steeping grain at 170°F.

Hops

0.5 ounces Perle Bittering hops are boiled for 90 minutes.

1 ounce Bog Myrtle is boiled for 90 minutes.

1 ounce Thyme is boiled for 5 minutes.

0.5 ounces Bog Myrtle is steeped for 10 minutes after wort boiling.

0.5 ounces Yarrow is steeped for 10 minutes after wort boiling.

1.5 ounces Labrador Tea is steeped for 10 minutes after wort boiling.

Wort Clarifying Treatment

Whirlfloc (use ½ to 1 Tablet) – Add at last 5 minutes of the boil.

KIT: ALL GRAIN

Grain

6.5 pounds Pilsner

4.15 pounds Vienna

1.18 pounds Munich

0.58 pounds CaraFoam

0.58 pounds Acidulated Malt

Boil for 90 minutes.

Recipe based on:
70% Mash Efficiency

Hops

0.5 ounces Perle Bittering hops are boiled for 90 minutes.

1 ounce Bog Myrtle is boiled for 90 minutes.

1 ounce thyme is boiled for 5 minutes.

0.5 ounces Bog Myrtle is steeped for 10 minutes after wort boiling.

0.5 ounces Yarrow is steeped for 10 minutes after wort boiling.

1.5 ounces Labrador Tea is steeped for 10 minutes after wort boiling.

Wort Clarifying Treatment

Whirlfloc (use ½ to 1 Tablet) – Add at last 5 minutes of the boil.

BURLEY OAK BREWING COMPANY

BERLIN MARYLAND

SOUR SAUCE
BERLINER WEISS

Bryan Brushmiller lost his job five days before Christmas in 2008. He was gutted—his life had been turned upside down in one unforgettable moment. He had no clue what he was going to do to feed his family. Looking back, it was a turning point in Brushmiller's life. During that time, he often retreated to his garage to do the only thing that stopped his worry, stress, and anxiety about the future. And that thing was brewing beer.

For the next year and a half, Brushmiller worked odd jobs and tried to write a business plan for what he thought was a pipe dream of starting a brewery in his small coastal community. Almost miraculously, those notepad sketches of what he wanted his brewery to be became tangible things and then realities. All of a sudden, he was a craft brewery advocate on the floor of the Maryland General Assembly in Annapolis fighting to change laws that would allow the dreams of other small brewers to also become real brick and mortar businesses. In the six years since Brushmiller opened the doors at Burley Oak Brewery in Berlin, Maryland, his team has released over 300 beers and built a following in an industry

that he never thought he would be a part of while brewing beers in his garage as an unemployed construction worker.

Brushmiller runs his business like it's a family because he ultimately sees all of its success as beneficial for his collective and actual family. To him, Burley Oak Brewery is just a larger version of his garage. Some of his favorite bands started in a garage, and some of the writers that changed his perspective on the world began in the most humble of places. For Brushmiller, it's incredibly gratifying to see something he dreamed up on a piece of notebook paper in his garage turn into something that means so much to his customers, his loyal and talented coworkers, and the future of his community. Since losing his job, Brushmiller's life has been turning lemons into lemonade, taking the road less travelled, and trying to create something that matters. He followed his passion, and in many ways, his passion saved him.

Sour Sauce represents the essence of being a small brewery owner: Sometimes, you start down one clearly defined path and end up somewhere else entirely. This beer is the perfect example of that. Burley Oak set out to make its Double IPA and halfway through the brewing process, its steam boiler broke in epic fashion. During that "oh shit" moment, the brewery was faced with either losing an entire batch of beer, or, for lack of a better cliché, trying to turn lemons into lemonade. Instead of abandoning the entire batch, the brew team quickly shifted gears to create one of the most sought-after sour beers that it's made to date.

The boiler had failed just after Burley Oak finished the runoff into the kettle. Without a way to boil the beer, it needed to buy some time. The decision was made to use *Lactobacillus delbrueckii*, a bacteria used in souring or acidifying beer. In doing this, the brewery was able to lower the pH of the beer over the weekend until the boiler technician could make a house call. As anyone in the industry will tell you, creative problem solving in harsh conditions and unfortunate situations is the epitome of good brewing and is a scenario that customers rarely see.

In spite of the decisive actions, Brushmiller wasn't overly optimistic about how the beer was going to turn out. It's rare for a sour beer to be 8 percent ABV, with a dark malt base, and no wood aging. Yet, when he tasted Sour Sauce for the first time, Brushmiller and his team were almost dumbfounded by the way the sweetness of the dark malts complemented the sour backbone. In the end, this beer's balance helped turn many Burley Oak customers on to sour beers. And in hindsight, Brushmiller thinks Sour Sauce is one of his brewery's most brilliant mistakes—the kind of mistake a small business owner can only dream of making.

	Extract	All Grain
Estimated original gravity (OG)	None Provided	None Provided
Estimated SRM		
Estimated IBU's		
Estimated alcohol ABV %		
Suggested fermentation temperature		

Specific Recipe Information

Follow a standard kettle sour procedure (i.e., two boils). Boil for 30 minutes after collecting wort in boil kettle. Chill wort to 115°F and pitch *Lactobacillus* strain of your choosing. Rest at 115°F for 3 days or until wort pH reaches desired acidity (tartness). Boil again for 90 minutes and add hops/sugar according to above schedule. The fermentation profile of your choosing can be used on this ale. We opted to do two separate things: The majority of wort was open fermented in a coolship collecting all sorts of wild yeasts and bacteria while a smaller portion was 100% oak barrel fermented to be released later in bottles.

If you are unable to open ferment, try cultivating some of your local flora on a petri dish, make a starter, and pitch that to your fermentor. Or, if that isn't possible, you could also buy a blend of yeasts and bacteria to create your own fermentation— have fun here as there are a lot of options in terms of brewing yeasts and bacteria. Remember: the art is in the fermentation!

KIT: EXTRACT

Malt Extracts/Additions

13 pounds Pale Malt Extract

Steeping Grain

8 ounces Honey Malt

8 ounces Munich Malt 10 L

Use a grain bag. Add to water immediately. Remove steeping grain at 170°F.

Hops

0.2 ounce Sterling

6.4 ounces table sugar

Bittering hops are boiled for 45 minutes.

Sugar is boiled for 30 minutes.

Wort Clarifying Treatment

KICK Carageenan (1 Tablet) – Add at last 5 minutes of the boil.

Bottling

4 ounces Corn Sugar – boil with 2 cups of water for 5 minutes.

KIT: ALL GRAIN

Grain

None Provided

CAMBRIDGE BREWING COMPANY
CAMBRIDGE MASSACHUSETTS

BULLPEN HIJINKS
GOSE

Internationally acclaimed and locally cherished, the Cambridge Brewing Company (CBC) has been at the forefront of the American craft brewery movement since its inception in 1989. Phil "Brewdaddy" Bannatyne traded a homebrewing hobby and a burgeoning party balloon business for the life of a brewer and restaurateur in a restored mill building near the Massachusetts Institute of Technology. One year after opening, Bannatyne hired Darryl Goss, an award-winning local homebrewer, to assist in the beer-making duties on the brewpub's ten-barrel system. At a time when most American brewers were attempting to replicate English ales or German lagers, Goss was fixated on the beer culture of Belgium. This fascination culminated in Tripel Threat—the first Belgian-style ale ever produced by an American brewer and the first Belgian-style beer to medal at the nascent Great American Beer Festival in 1991, long before a Belgian category existed in the competition—and set the trajectory for the little brewery to produce extraordinarily creative beers.

Will Meyers, CBC's brewmaster for the past twenty years, joined the roster in 1993 as another local homebrewer-gone-pro, and together, the three brewers focused on then-unusual beers like authentic Bavarian Hefeweizen, Belgian Saison, unhopped Gruit ales, and Finnish Sahti, in addition to pale ale and porter. In a time before the Internet and without the resources of information and ingredients available today, this was truly groundbreaking brewing.

Under Meyers' direction, CBC became one of the first U.S. breweries to create a barrel-aging program where "wild" fermentations with *Brettanomyces* and intentionally sour beers aged in Solera systems were created alongside bourbon barrel-aged stouts and experimental barleywine interpretations of Sauternes. CBC's creative influences come not only from the greater brewing world but also largely from music and other creative arts. Like Paul McCartney's "Yesterday," sometimes inspiration literally strikes in a dream, as in CBC's experimental beer Benevolence. And for other beers, much like in songwriting, sometimes the lyrics come first, other times it's the melody. And sometimes, a title alone is enough to inspire the song.

End of day beers with the brewing team invariably lead to discussions on new ingredients, fermentation techniques, bad puns, and good-natured busting on other beers and pop culture. At any moment, a great idea for a new beer may emerge from the banter. Sometimes, a potentially awesome beer name results—unique beer names are getting harder and harder to invent these days—to which the crew decides to design the beer itself. Occasionally, a beer will remain unnamed until the moment it's ready to be tapped, prompting Meyers to accost staff members and customers alike with Allen Ginsberg's phrase "First thought, best thought."

Bullpen Hijinks is a Leipzig Gose-style beer inspired by an ingredient and facilitated by a collaboration with Valley Malt, local craft maltsters in Hadley, Massachusetts. A discussion on waste streams and how they can be used as potential beer ingredients led to sunflower oil production and the leftover meal, typically sold as animal feed. But when early experiments with the roasted, pelletized sunflower meal offered unsatisfactory results, Andrea Stanley of Valley Malt offered to malt the seeds herself. CBC received the pilot batch of sunflower malt, and as the staff happily munched most of them, conversations about summertime, baseball, salted sunflower seeds, and logically, Gosebier, ensued.

Meyers and CBC brewers Alex Corona and Kevin Dwyer met to homebrew a pilot batch using the malted sunflower seeds along with a traditional grist of malted barley and malted wheat. Yogurt was employed as the souring culture for the beer's natural acidity via kettle wort souring, and the light addition of salt to the wort completed the palate of toasted, salted sunflower seeds in this tart, dry beer. The first full-scale batch was brewed for BeerAdvocate's Microbrew Invitational beer festival held in Boston in June 2016, and the name was chosen for its ability to evoke sunflower seed spitting contests and the general goofy hijinks of the Boston Red Sox pitching squad.

	Extract	All Grain
Estimated original gravity (OG)	1.040	1.040
Estimated SRM		
Estimated IBU's		
Estimated alcohol ABV %	4%	4%
Suggested fermentation temperature	68 to 70°F	68 to 70°F

Specific Recipe Information

This beer features anaerobically soured wort in the kettle, prior to boiling and fermentation. In advance, purchase very fresh plain yogurt labeled "live active cultures" or order pure *Lactobacillus* cultures from a yeast lab.

Dilute malt extract in warm water, raise to 150°F, and add crushed specialty malts and sunflower seeds in a mesh bag. Soak 30 minutes and remove, draining thoroughly, and boil 5 minutes to sterilize wort. Purge your lidded brew kettle with CO_2 at 1 psi to remove air.

Using a sanitized heat exchanger, cool to 100°F, and measure wort pH. Insulate kettle to maintain temperature. Draw off 16 ounces warm wort and whisk 6 ounces of yogurt. Add to wort in kettle. Over the next 24 to 36 hours, re-santize your whisk, low-flow CO_2 purge the kettle, and stir wort to maintain cultures in suspension. Monitor wort pH and temperature. Things are going well when the wort begins to smell like pineapple juice! With wort pH at 3.4 to 3.8, place kettle back on heat source and boil.

Boil 90 minutes, with additions of hops, coriander, and salt. Cool wort, add to fermentor, oxygenate, and pitch a very strong active starter of neutral yeast such as London Ale or California Ale yeast.

KIT: EXTRACT

Malt Extracts/Additions

5 pounds Wheat Malt Extract syrup

2 pounds Pale Malt Extract syrup

Turn burner off before adding Liquid Malt Extract.

Steeping Grain

0.25 pounds Melanoidin Malt

0.15 pounds Acid Malt

2 pounds malted sunflower seeds, cracked OR

2 pounds roasted unsalted sunflower seeds, cracked

Use a grain bag. Add to wort at 150°F. Remove steeping grain after 30 minutes.

Hops

0.75 ounces Hallertauer at 60 minutes.

14 grams ground coriander at 5 minutes.

18 grams sea salt at 5 minutes.

Wort Clarifying Treatment

Whirlfloc (use ½ to 1 Tablet) – Add at last 5 minutes of the boil.

KIT: ALL GRAIN

Grain

6 pounds Wheat Malt

3 pounds 2 Row

0.25 pounds Melanoidin Malt

0.15 pounds Acid Malt

2 pounds malted sunflower seeds, cracked OR

2 pounds roasted unsalted sunflower seeds, cracked

0.75 ounces Hallertauer at 60 minutes.

14 grams ground coriander at 5 minutes.

1 gram sea salt at 5 minutes.

Recipe based on: 70% Mash Efficiency

Strike Water Temperature: °F

Mash Temperature: 149°F

Time: 60 minutes

Sparge Water Temperature: 170°F

Time:

Wort Clarifying Treatment:

Whirlfloc (use ½ to 1 Tablet) – Add at last 5 minutes of the boil.

CAPTAIN LAWRENCE BREWING COMPANY

**ELMSFORD
NEW YORK**

Beer Name

NOR`EASTER
BELGIAN STRONG DARK ALE

Captain Lawrence brewing got its start like a lot of small breweries do, with its founder, Scott Vaccaro, brewing five gallons (19 L) of beer on the top of a kitchen stove at his home on Captain Lawrence Drive, in the suburbs of New York. And while homebrewing is no big feat these days, doing it at age seventeen is still something you don't hear about often. That first brew out of *The Complete Joy of Homebrewing*, Charlie Papazian's homebrewing "Bible," lit the fire that was needed to start a lifelong journey in search of the illusive perfect pint of beer.

Ten years after that initial batch of homebrew, Vaccaro brewed the first commercial batch of Captain Lawrence beer in Pleasantville, New York, in December of 2005. Located in a 5,800 square foot (539 square meter) warehouse with a small tasting room, the brewery was built out of a bunch of used equipment cobbled together from some defunct breweries and others that had just outgrown their tanks and tools. The goal was to brew and deliver beer to Westchester County and sell what was left out of the tasting room. Small dreams and goals that would change and grow with every day that passed.

Three short months after opening the brewery, the tasting room was set to debut on a cold day in February. Within a few minutes of opening, a crowd overwhelmed the small room and spilled out into the brewery. It quickly became clear that people in the area had been waiting for a brewery to open and the demand for locally brewed beer was real, not just an entrepreneur's dream.

After outgrowing the Pleasantville space in early 2011, the build-out of the current brewery site began. Located only four miles (6 km) south, the new home of Captain Lawrence Brewing in Elmsford is more than four times the size of the original space. Housing two bottling lines, a forty-barrel automated brewhouse, a separate barrel aging room and over 3,000 square foot (279 square meter) of tasting room and patio space, the new facility is built for growth.

More than a decade later, Captain Lawrence is still focusing on its original reason for brewing: the search for intensity of flavor and the never-ending diversity of style. Brewing everything from 10 percent ABV barrel-aged sour ales to 4 percent ABV session lagers, the journey founder Scott Vaccaro started as a teenager lives on in the Hudson Valley.

Originally brewed in the winter of 2008, this beer takes a few of the brewery team's favorite styles and mashes them up into a very drinkable, flavorful beverage that is dark and roasty, strong and fruity, and layered and intriguing.

The body is based loosely on an Imperial stout recipe. For this beer, the roasted character is kept in check a little more than expected with less roasted barely and dark malt than is typical in a stout. The goal is to come close to 10 percent ABV with the recipe's traditional malt bill portion. Then, a Belgian yeast strain acts as the heart, creating flavors in conjunction with the roasted malts that make drinking Nor' Easter a truly unique experience. Using a Belgian strain that can handle the alcohol production and won't stop before a complete fermentation is very important. Finally, there's the soul—this beer takes on an entirely new identity when the elderberry syrup is added to kick off a secondary fermentation, adding both more alcohol and a vinous, strong flavor that adds another layer of intensity. Tying it all together with layers of char and vanilla are the bourbon barrels this beer ages in.

	Extract	All Grain
Estimated original gravity (OG)	1.100	None Provided
Estimated SRM		
Estimated IBU's	55	
Estimated alcohol ABV %	11.5%	
Suggested fermentation temperature	75°F	

Specific Recipe Information

After fermentation has reached 2 degree plato above terminal gravity, create your elderberry syrup.

Mix cane sugar at a rate of 1.5 pounds/gallon water, bring to boil, and add in elderberries. Allow to steep overnight before adding to the fermenter. This should kick off another round of fermentation and add a ton of flavor and intensity.

Ferment with Belgian-style Ale yeast.

Age the beer in bourbon barrels for one month or on oak chips soaked in bourbon.

KIT: EXTRACT

Malt Extracts/Additions

15 pounds Dark Malt Extract

1.5 pounds cane sugar

0.5 pounds elderberries

Turn burner off before adding. Boil for 60 minutes.

Steeping Grain

1 pound Roasted Barley

1 pound Special B Malt

Use a grain bag. Add to water immediately. Remove steeping grain at 170°F.

Hops

1.75 ounces CTZ

Looking for 55 IBU

Boil for 60 minutes

Wort Clarifying Treatment

Whirlfloc (use ½ to 1 Tablet) – Add at last 5 minutes of the boil.

KIT: ALL GRAIN

Grain

78% 2-Row Pale

8.5% Dark Munich

8.5% Dark Crystal 120 L

4% Wyermann Carafa III

0.5% Roasted Barley

10% cane sugar

0.10 pounds/gallon elderberries

Turn burner off before adding. Boil for 60 minutes.

Recipe based on: 70% Mash Efficiency

Strike Water Temperature: 155°F

Mash Temperature: 152°F

Time: 30 minutes

Sparge Water Temperature: 170°F

Looking for 55 IBU

Boil for 60 minutes

Wort Clarifying Treatment

Whirlfloc (use ½ to 1 Tablet) – Add at last 5 minutes of the boil.

CARTON BREWING COMPANY

ATLANTIC HIGHLANDS NEW JERSEY

Carton Brewing debuted to the beer-drinking public over the summer of 2011, back when session IPA was a contradiction in terms, not a beer style. To founders Augie and Chris Carton, such dissimilarity was a creative opportunity, an opening to join the widening craft brewing conversation by offering a peerless beer that would also be a defining moment.

The beer, dubbed Boat, satisfied the cousins' quest for a robustly hopped, low-alcohol ale that remained complex and interesting from first sip to last, without getting a person wrecked after a few pints. For craft brewing, it was a new frontier, one that answered the question of how to stuff a ton of hops into a little beer and still keep it real. For Carton Brewing, it was the first step on a path committed to innovation, a path to what they call "Off the Beaten Craft."

To that end, and to make tasty beer in the place where their tastes were forged, Augie and Chris Carton tricked out a turn-of-the-twentieth century, red-brick warehouse in the New Jersey seashore community where they were born and raised. And when the cousins set the first pints of Boat in front of a hometown bar crowd on a stormy August night six years ago, they opened a new channel in craft brewing that would ultimately become the well-stocked session IPA category.

Since then, the brewery has built a reputation for pushing boundaries with ingredients and pushing the possibilities of what beer can be, creating unique brews that confirm beer's role as cuisine, while simultaneously demonstrating that cuisine can be beer. But Carton Brewing's story will always be about leading off with that groundbreaking, hoppy session ale, made with the guiding thought that no one should have to leave their stomping ground to find beers that wow and excite. After all, your hometown is the place you insist has the best burger, the best coffee, the best bagel, and the best pizza (or you should move), so why shouldn't the best beer be part of that boast?

Beer Name

DELI
FLANDERS RED

For *Project Extreme Brewing*, Carton's ambition was to have fun with all five tastes (bitter, salty, sweet, sour, and umami) with something simple, classic, and unique to the Mid-Atlantic region. Starting with the archetypal pastrami sandwich, on rye, with a kosher pickle, Carton deconstructed and reassembled it as a beer that tastes like a beer while evoking the aspects that make that sandwich combination exceptional. For the unctuousness of seasoned brisket, Carton uses a Flanders Red foundation.

Over time and slow exposure to wood, Flanders Red develops richness like few beers. The saltiness of the pastrami cure is what ultimately ties the myriad flavors together, so Carton salted the wort enough to allow the other elements to pop. On the plate, the pickle, the vinegary mustard, and that light sour touch in the crumb of good rye bread accentuate the flavors of the rich, peppery meat. The inherent sourness of the beer, lightly seasoned with the dill qualities of Sorachi Ace hops, mustard seeds, and rye malts before flame out, with some fresh dill as a dry hop, bend the beer's sour to the dish's notions. In the dish, the sweetness is as simple as sugar in the rub and good bread. In the beer, brown sugar dries it out, leaving some treacle aromas behind, while Special B, CaraMunich, and Aroma malt give enough uniting sweetness without becoming cloying. Pronounced black pepper, paprika, mustard, and caraway give the sandwich bitterness. Here, they go in at flame out, allowing the spices to cook and be present throughout the palate rather than overbearing at the end. Carton also adds smoked malt to the grist as an acrid touch and for its general evocation of meatiness.

Suggested Fermentation Schedule

Wyeast 1056 at 68°F for 2 weeks plus

Wyeast 3763 at 68°F for 12 months

Specific Recipe Information

Place un-milled steeping grains in a grain bag. Add the grain bag to 2 gallons of 150°F water. Allow grain bag (which will float) to steep for 20 to 30 minutes while you continue to heat the water up to no hotter than 170°F, in order to avoid extracting tannins.

Next, remove the grain bag, top your kettle up with enough preheated water to reach a total pre-boil volume of 8 gallons, and turn your heat source back on. Once you reach a boil, add your malt extract and hops. After adding the extract, your preboil gravity should be 1.047 SG. Add kettle finings with 10 minutes remaining in the boil.

After the boil, turn off the heat and add ¼ cup of the pastrami spice blend. Whirlpool the kettle by gently stirring with a spoon or mash paddle for 2 minutes and then let rest for an additional 18 minutes to achieve a 20-minute flame out steep. Next, chill the wort to 66°F and transfer into a clean and sanitized fermenter. Aerate the wort with pure oxygen for 60 seconds and pitch Wyeast 1056. Ferment at 68°F for 2 weeks, transfer to a CO_2 purged secondary fermenter, and then pitch Wyeast 3763. Condition at 68°F for 12 months, preferably in an oak barrel (or add 1.5 ounces of oak cubes for the last 3 conditioning months) and then dry hop with ¼ cup of fresh dill before carbonating and packaging.

	Extract	All Grain
Estimated original gravity (OG)	1.056	1.030–1.040
Estimated SRM	13	2–3
Estimated IBU's	19	7–10
Estimated alcohol ABV %	6.6%	4.5%
Suggested fermentation temperature		68°F

NOTE: If bottle conditioning, add 2 to 3 grams of USO5 dry yeast along with 3.75 ounces of priming sugar and allow bottles to prime in a 68°F room for 3 to 4 weeks, or direct carbonate in a keg to 2.5 volumes of CO_2. FAST APPROACH: If you don't want to use Wyeast 3763, a fun alternative is to add (to taste) pasteurized malt vinegar and additional spice blend (make a neutral spirit tincture) to the batch at packaging and then condition the beer to taste (3 to 6 months generally). You should also only use ⅛ cup of pastrami spice blend in the whirlpool to account for the shorter conditioning period.

KIT: EXTRACT

Malt Extracts/Additions

3.75 pounds Briess CBW Rye LME
Boil for 60 minutes.

Steeping Grain

0.75 pounds Beechwood Smoked Malt
0.375 pounds Dingemans Special B Malt
0.375 pounds Castle Aroma Malt
Use a grain bag. Add to water immediately. Remove steeping grain at 170°F.

Hops

0.5 ounces Sorachi Ace (13% AA)

Pastrami Spice Blend Proportions and Preparation

0.5 tbsp Indian coriander
2 tbsp yellow mustard seed
2 tbsp lightly packed dark brown sugar
1 tbsp smoked paprika
1 tbsp dill seed
1 tsp caraway seed
1 tsp kosher salt
⅛ tsp granulated garlic
⅛ tsp ground cloves
2 tbsp coarsely ground black pepper

Toast coriander and mustard seeds in a medium skillet over medium heat, stirring occasionally, until fragrant and lightly browned (3 to 5 minutes). Transfer to small bowl to cool. Add the cooled seeds, sugar, paprika, salt, garlic, dill, caraway, and cloves to a spice grinder and grind to the texture of dry sand. Transfer to a small bowl and stir in the pepper. Keep in an airtight container at room temperature in a dry place away from sunlight for up to 3 months.

Wort Clarifying Treatment

Whirlfloc (½ Tablet) – Add at last 10 minutes of the boil.

KIT: ALL GRAIN

Grain

5 pounds German Pilsner Malt
3.25 pounds Vienna Malt
2.25 pounds Rye Malt
1 pound Beechwood Smoked Malt
0.75 pounds Weyerman Munich I Malt
0.5 pounds Dingemans Special B Malt
0.5 pounds CaraMunich Malt
0.5 pounds Castle Aroma Malt
Recipe based on: 78% Mash Efficiency
Strike Water Temperature: 166°F
Mash Temperature: 153°F
Time: 60 minutes
Sparge Water Temperature: 167°F

Preboil Volume: 8 gallons
Preboil Gravity: 1.047
Boil Length: 60 minutes
Postboil Volume: 7 gallons
Postboil Gravity: 1.056
Batch Size: 6 gallons in fermenter
Brewhouse Efficiency: 70%

Pastrami Spice Blend Proportions and Preparation

See extract

Hops

0.5 ounces Sorachi Ace (13% AA)

Wort Clarifying Treatment

Whirlfloc (½ Tablet) – Add at last 10 minutes of the boil.

DUE SOUTH BREWING COMPANY

BOYNTON BEACH FLORIDA

Beer Name

ONE NIGHT IN YBOR

BARREL-AGED SCOTCH ALE

Mike and Jodi Halker founded Due South Brewing Company in 2011. Although it wasn't that long ago, there were very few breweries in Florida at the time. While the landscape for well-made craft beer continued to grow in the rest of America, Florida, and particularly South Florida, lagged behind. Recognizing the need for real independent beer in this area, the couple decided to open Due South in Boynton Beach.

After spending months changing various municipal codes in conjunction with city officials to allow an operating brewery within city limits, Due South finally found a home in a 15,000 square foot (1,394 square meter) warehouse in an industrial area around the corner from I-95. On May 12, 2012, Due South opened its doors to the public. Always focused on production, the location was nothing fancy, just a big open warehouse where people could have a beer next to the folks who were making it. The original seating plan called for thirty-two seats for taproom customers, but within a few months, it had grown to seating for over 160 as locals continued showing up to find out what real beer was all about.

Due South began to distribute in the South Florida area soon after opening, limiting distribution to just three counties. As the area's first production-focused brewery, no one knew quite what to expect. All of the beer was produced on a fifteen-barrel brewhouse and capacity was limited to five fermenters under thirty barrels. Within two years, Due South would add six, sixty-barrel fermenters, increase production to almost 5,000 barrels per year, expand distribution from Key West to Jacksonville, and take home the Best Large Brewery award in the Best Florida Beer competition. And Due South continues to grow, most recently adding the 12,000 square foot (1,115 square meter) space next door to house a new taproom and increase its production area.

While Due South is known for its flagship beers Caramel Cream Ale and Category 3 IPA, the brewery typically produces between 60 and 100 beers per year, pushing boundaries with offerings such as Mexican Standoff (a robust porter with habanero chilies, bakers chocolate, and cinnamon) and Calling All Cars, a coffee and doughnut porter. Plus, accomplishments like pulling off a fifty-tap takeover in one night at the World of Beer in Wellington, Florida, prove the folks at Due South love what they do.

One Night in Ybor is a modification on a strong Scotch ale brewed to showcase the flavors of the classic Old Fashioned cocktail. Named after a particularly eventful evening in Tampa's Ybor City area that involved a few of the brewers and a great deal of whiskey, bitters, oranges, and cherries, this beer was designed the next day on the three and a half hour van ride home from Ybor to Due South. With a Scotch ale already aging in Woodford Reserve bourbon barrels, the remaining ingredients were sourced: Bing cocktail cherries and fresh Florida orange peel zested right before adding

The first attempt was done in a firkin using priming sugar. A few days later, arriving back at the brewery around midnight after an event at a local bar, the crew found the firkin had burst, blowing cherries across the building over 100 feet (30.5 m). In fact, most of the brewery and taproom were covered with cherries and beer. After an extended clean up, some additional math determined the cause of the explosion—they had mistakenly failed to add the sugar content of the cherries to the calculations. Keep this in mind if you plan to bottle condition this beer. Subsequent batches at Due South haven't had this issue (although, to be safe, firkins are now conditioned in containers with lids), and One Night in Ybor remains one of the most in-demand beers in the brewery's lineup.

	Extract	All Grain
Estimated original gravity (OG)	1.077	None Provided
Estimated SRM	19.7	
Estimated IBU's	21.1	
Estimated alcohol ABV %	8.2%	
Suggested fermentation temperature	66 to 68°F	

Specific Recipe Information

Add 1 pound of corn sugar the last 5 minutes of the boil. Soak 3 ounces of oak chips in bourbon for 3 days prior to adding to secondary.

In secondary, add oak chips and bourbon, 13.5 ounce jar of bing cherries, zest from 3 oranges, and 1 dash of bitters.

Bottle or keg after treating one week in secondary.

If bottling: Add 3 ounces corn sugar and boil with 2 cups of water for 5 minutes.

KIT: EXTRACT

Malt Extracts/Additions

8 pounds Light DME

Turn burner off before adding. Boil for 60 minutes.

Steeping Grain

6 ounces Munich

6 ounces Carapils

4 ounces Crystal 120L

4 ounces Chocolate Malt

3 ounces Black Malt

3 ounces Smoked Malt

Use a grain bag. Add to water immediately. Remove steeping grain at 170°F.

Hops

1.5 ounces East Kent Goldings

Bittering Hops are boiled for 60 minutes.

Wort Clarifying Treatment

Whirlfloc (use ½ to 1 Tablet) – Add at last 5 minutes of the boil.

KIT: ALL GRAIN

Grain

12 pounds 2-Row

6 ounces Munich

6 ounces Carapils

4 ounces Crystal 120L

4 ounces Chocolate Malt

3 ounces Black Malt

3 ounces Smoked Malt

Recipe based on:
70% Mash Efficiency

Hops

1.5 ounces East Kent Goldings

Bittering Hops are boiled for 60 minutes.

Wort Clarifying Treatment

Whirlfloc (use ½ to 1 Tablet) – Add at last 5 minutes of the boil.

EARTH EAGLE BREWINGS

PORTSMOUTH
NEW HAMPSHIRE

PUCA
PUMPKIN
PORTER

The story of Earth Eagle Brewings began in November of 2012. After a few years of homebrewing during which medals were won and friends and family were wowed, Butch Heilshorn and Alex McDonald opened Portsmouth, New Hampshire's second brewery. The plan was to brew the beers they wanted to drink, some of which they had never even tasted before.

Not only was Earth Eagle Portsmouth's second brewpub, its one-barrel capacity made it one of the smallest commercial breweries in New England. The big benefit to brewing on such a small system was the ability to brew lots of different recipes. Heilshorn and McDonald set out to brew well-executed traditional styles alongside unusual beer with unusual ingredients, and four years later, they are still concocting new, creative, and tasty beers.

With the popularity of their beer quickly growing, it soon became apparent that the one-barrel brewery could not keep up with the demands on their business. So, the young company doubled the size of their brewhouse shortly after opening. A series of expansions in their serving area and kitchen followed, and currently, Earth Eagle seats forty-four people for lunch and dinner and features a full bar as well as guest taps. The company has an extremely limited distribution program in New Hampshire, Massachusetts, and Maine, primarily designed to entice customers to visit their cozy Portsmouth brewpub.

Earth Eagle Brewings keeps growing today and continues to delight in redefining the boundaries of brewing. From re-creations of historical beers such as seventeenth-century Mumme and a similarly obscure Cock Ale, to solid IPAs and Belgians, to never-before-brewed Gruits with locally foraged roots, fruits, flowers, and leaves, the brewery has stuck to its motto of making "empyreal ales and wonder Gruits."

In a world of pumpkin spiced beers reminiscent of Thanksgiving pie, Puca (poo-kah) was born to be different. The "Puca" is primarily a creature of Irish folklore said to be a shape shifter that usually takes the form of black horses, goats, and sometimes human beings with animal features such as long ears and tails. Worshiped during the harvest season, the last of the year's crops were left in the fields as the Puca's share.

Earth Eagle celebrates the season's change and the fall harvest by brewing a few batches of its curry pumpkin porter. The idea came from the curry pumpkin soups that Alex McDonald had been making for years and the thought that the flavors in them would balance beautifully with a rich porter. The addition of curry powder and Thai chilies gives a nice touch of heat to the delicate chocolate character and the sweetness of the malt. And the rum-soaked coconut? Well, that's just icing on the cake.

	Extract	All Grain
Estimated original gravity (OG)	1.064	1.064
Estimated SRM	29	29
Estimated IBU's	34.9	34.9
Estimated alcohol ABV %	7%	7%
Suggested fermentation temperature	68°F	68°F

Specific Recipe Information

Cut 5 pounds of sugar pumpkins into chucks and cook until soft (making a pumpkin tea); strain the water and use in your boil. Cover and soak 1 pound unsweetened shaved coconut in dark rum of your choice for at least 24 hours. Add coconut shavings to secondary or after fermentation is complete. Allow 1 week before bottling or kegging. Use 5 ounces of corn sugar for bottling.

KIT: EXTRACT

Malt Extracts/Additions

6.6 pounds Light Liquid Malt Extract

1 pound Light Dry Malt Extract

1 pound coconut sugar

Heat to boil. Turn burner off before adding. Return to boil for 60 minutes.

Steeping Grain

4 ounces Carafa III

4 ounces Chocolate Malt

4 ounces Black Malt

4 ounces Special B Malt

Use a grain bag. Add 2 gallons of water and heat to 160°F. Add grains and steep at 150°F for 20 minutes.

Hops

0.5 ounces Sorachi Ace at 60 minutes.

0.5 ounce Sorachi Ace at 15 minutes.

1 ounce Amarillo at 5 minutes.

0.25 ounce curry powder at 0 minutes.

8 ounces Thai chili peppers at 0 minutes.

Wort Clarifying Treatment

Whirlfloc (use ½ to 1 Tablet) – Add at last 5 minutes of the boil.

KIT: ALL GRAIN

Grain

9 pounds Maris Otter

2 pounds Munich

0.25 pounds Carafa III

0.25 pounds Black Malt

0.25 pounds Chocolate Malt

0.25 pounds Special B Malt

5 pounds fresh sugar pumpkin (Chopped)

Recipe based on:
70% Mash Efficiency

Strike Water Temperature: 160°F

Mash Temperature: 150°F

Time: 60 minutes

Sparge Water Temperature: 170°F

Time: 60 minutes

Hops

Boil for 60 minutes.

1 pound coconut sugar

0.5 ounces Sorachi Ace (First Wort)

0.5 ounces Sorachi Ace at 15 minutes.

1 ounce Amarillo at 5 minutes.

0.25 ounces curry powder

0.5 pounds Thai chili peppers

Wort Clarifying Treatment

Whirlfloc (use ½ to 1 Tablet) – Add at last 5 minutes of the boil.

FINBACK BREWERY

RIDGEWOOD
NEW YORK

THE KNOWN UNIVERSE

GOSE

● ●

Finback began as a dream to combine two obsessions: beer and creativity. Achieving this dream in New York City was also important, though, so maybe it should be three obsessions. Cofounders Basil Lee and Kevin Stafford both had creative backgrounds and a passion for unique, delicious beers and set out on a three-year mission to open a brewery in New York City. After clearing many hurdles and nearly giving up, Finback finally became a reality in 2014, opening in the borough of Queens.

Starting a brewery in New York City poses many challenges, but fortunately, the city has a strong beer drinking and brewing community. At the time, a few well-established breweries in the city paved the way for a string of new, small, and passionate younger breweries. So, with sheer determination, Finback became one of the first in this new wave of breweries. Their collective mantra was "by any means necessary" and together they continue to build a dynamic community of exceptional brewing companies, establishing the city as a serious beer destination.

Although small, Finback was deeply committed to brewing a wide array of rotating styles. The brewery's philosophy is to take style as a starting point and build interesting flavors and combinations, experiment with unusual ingredients, and to push creativity. In a short period of time, Finback has brewed over eighty beers ranging from hoppy IPAs and fruited sours to barrel-aged stouts and Brett beers. Through collaborations, both internally and with other breweries and friends, Finback is always searching for something different and delicious.

From the outset, Finback was committed to creating a barrel-aging program. Starting with only two bourbon barrels, the brewery has accumulated nearly 300 barrels to date, including red and white wine, bourbon, apple brandy, and rum barrels. The addition of foeders has allowed for even more aging and beers with greater complexity. One of the first barrel-aged beers Finback brewed was BQE Imperial Stout, a celebration of the boroughs the founders lived and worked in: Brooklyn and Queens. Made with cacao nibs from Brooklyn and coffee roasted and brewed in Queens, this Imperial stout was the fifth beer ever brewed at the brewery and went into the first bourbon barrels they could afford. Released at the end of 2014, BQE became one of Finback's most sought-after brews and is now brewed annually.

The Known Universe is a Gose brewed with Calamansi and chili. Gose, a historic German style invented in Leipzig, is a refreshing drink anytime, but particularly in the summer, being a dry, sour, and salty brew. Like its German cousin Berliner Weisse, Gose was sometimes spiked with a shot of fruit syrup to balance the beer's acidity and salinity. Finback was inspired by this tradition and incorporated Calamansi, which is a sweet and sour citrus fruit. Likely a hybrid between mandarin orange and kumquat, Calamansi has a wonderful orange, tangelo flavor with bright sour notes. Adding a kick of spice—in this case Habanero pepper—makes for an extra refreshing beer.

The Known Universe is brewed with 2-row malt, a variation on the Pilsner typically used for the base malt, which gives the beer a touch more color and structure. Another difference is the absence of coriander, allowing the chili and Calamansi to shine independently. If you're lucky enough to know someone with a Calamansi tree or can find it fresh, use that. Otherwise, a good frozen puree will work or, if necessary, substitute another tart citrus. A touch of rye malt is also added to augment the spice from Habanero chili.

	Extract	All Grain
Estimated original gravity (OG)	1.048–1.050	1.030–1.040
Estimated SRM	5	2–3
Estimated IBU's	6–9	7–10
Estimated alcohol ABV %	5.2%	4.5%
Suggested fermentation temperature	68°F	68°F

Specific Recipe Information

Transfer wort to kettle and boil for 10 minutes to sterilize. Cool to 100°F and inoculate with *Lactobacillus* for 1 to 2 days maintaining temperature–pH should lower to 3.3–3.5. After pH is lowered, boil for 60 minutes and add hops as normal. When fermentation is complete, puree. 0.5 pounds of calamansi lime, 1 habanero and add to secondary. Priming Sugar: 4.2 ounces corn sugar – Boil with 2 cups of water for 5 minutes.

KIT: EXTRACT

Malt Extracts/Additions

5 pounds Light Malt Extract

1 pound Wheat Malt Extract

20 grams sea salt

Turn burner off before adding. Boil for 60 minutes.

Steeping Grain

8 ounces Rye malt

8 ounces Acidulated Malt

8 ounces Flaked Oats

Use a grain bag. Add to water immediately. Remove steeping grain at 170°F.

Hops

0.2 ounces Summit

Bittering/flavoring hops boiled the last 20 minutes.

Wort Clarifying Treatment

Whirlfloc (use ½ to 1 Tablet) – Add at last 5 minutes of the boil.

KIT: ALL GRAIN

Grain

7 pounds 2-Row

24 ounces Wheat Malt

8 ounces Rye Malt

8 ounces Acidulated Malt

8 ounces Flaked Oats

20 grams sea salt

Turn burner off before adding. Boil for 60 minutes.

Recipe based on: 70% Mash Efficiency

Strike Water Temperature: N/A

Mash Temperature: 184°F

Time: 60 minutes

Sparge Water Temperature: N/A

Hops

0.2 ounces Summit

Bittering/flavoring hops are boiled the last 20 minutes.

Wort Clarifying Treatment

Whirlfloc (use ½ to 1 Tablet) – Add at last 5 minutes of the boil.

FOOLPROOF BREWING COMPANY

**PAWTUCKET
RHODE ISLAND**

SHUCKOLATE

**CHOCOLATE-OYSTER
STOUT**

After pursuing his dream of opening a new brewery in Rhode Island for several years, Nick Garrison founded Foolproof Brewing Company in 2012. Like most people in the brewing industry, Garrison started his career as an avid homebrewer. After only a few months of making his own tasty brews that included brewing all of the beer for his wedding, Garrison quickly realized that what had started as a hobby had quickly spiraled into an obsession. Determined to turn his dream of owning a brewery into a reality, Garrison set out to put together a plan and a team. Partnering with the company's original brewmaster, Damase Olsson, the Pawtucket-based brewery started brewing in December of 2012.

The company quickly expanded its operations and its distribution footprint across New England, and now, amid its third expansion, Foolproof has grown to become the largest brewery in the state of Rhode Island. The brewery continues to grow under Garrison's leadership with brewing operations currently led by head brewer Steve Sharp. Today, Foolproof's beers are distributed in all six New England states as well as Houston, Texas. The company brews five year-round beers as well as six specialty beers, with more in planning for the future.

At Foolproof, beer is treated as an experience that should be thoroughly savored and enjoyed. Foolproof takes specific life experiences, moods, seasons, and even weather and pairs them with beer styles fitting for those particular occasions. With this concept of "experience-based brewing," each beer serves as a tribute to a cherished beer drinking moment—whether it's watching a baseball game, relaxing at home on a rainy day, or just catching up with friends at the local pub, Foolproof's goal is to create a unique and fulfilling beer experience for its customers.

Although the company started out brewing fairly traditional styles like porter, IPA, and golden ale, with Steve Sharp at the helm of brewing operations, Foolproof has since ventured into more extreme styles of beer that are creating a buzz. The company's Peanut Butter Raincloud Porter, Shuckolate Chocolate-Oyster Stout, and Queen of the Yahd Raspberry IPA have grown to become some of its most popular offerings and are popping up in bars and liquor stores all over New England. Shuckolate in particular represents a noteworthy venture into the realm of extreme brewing. With plans to release a beer around Valentine's Day, Foolproof's team devised a recipe featuring two traditional aphrodisiacs (oysters and chocolate) and partnered with two local companies to brew a stout unlike anything available in its home market. Shuckolate remains a favorite among chocolate and oyster lovers and is one of the brewery's most popular offerings at its tasting room in Pawtucket.

	Extract	All Grain
Estimated original gravity (OG)	1.061	1.061
Estimated SRM	38	38
Estimated IBU's	32	32
Estimated alcohol ABV %	6%	6%
Suggested fermentation temperature	68°F	68°F

Specific Recipe Information

Add 1 pound of cocoa powder to the mash.

Add 5 whole oysters for the last 15 minutes of the boil.

Add 1 pound of cocoa nibs to the fermenter after one week in primary.

KIT: EXTRACT

Malt Extracts/Additions

6.8 pounds Dry malt extract-light

Steeping Grain

8 ounces Crystal 40 L

4 ounces Carafa III

4 ounces Roasted Barley

4 ounces Chocolate Wheat

4 ounces Chocolate Rye

4 ounces Chocolate Malt

Use a grain bag. Add to water immediately. Remove steeping grain at 170°F.

Hops

0.5 ounces Nugget—boil for 60 minutes.

0.25 ounces Nugget—boil for 45 minutes.

Wort Clarifying Treatment

Whirlfloc (use ½ to 1 Tablet) – Add at last 5 minutes of the boil.

KIT: ALL GRAIN

Grain

9.5 pounds 2-Row

8 ounces Crystal 40 L

4 ounces Carafa III

4 ounces Roasted Barley

4 ounces Chocolate Wheat

4 ounces Chocolate Rye

4 ounces Chocolate Malt

Recipe based on:
75% Mash Efficiency

Hops

0.5 ounces Nugget—boil for 60 minutes.

0.25 ounces Nugget—boil for 45 minutes.

Wort Clarifying Treatment

Whirlfloc (use ½ to 1 Tablet) – Add at last 5 minutes of the boil.

FORBIDDEN ROOT RESTAURANT & BREWERY

CHICAGO
ILLINOIS

Forbidden Root, Chicago's first botanic brewery, brews craft beer inspired by nature. It uses barley, water, hops, and yeast as a base to explore a rich world of wild ingredients like bark, stems, flowers, herbs, spices, leaves, roots, and other foraged flavors that have long been part of beer. Brewers in early America crafted low-alcohol beverages, infusing them with botanicals like ginger, dandelion, burdock, and other plants available to them. Unfortunately, by the early twentieth century, botanic brews were largely displaced by carbonated sodas produced industrially without fermentation. Forbidden Root views this early brewing tradition as a springboard for great creativity and exploration. So while Forbidden Root didn't invent botanic beer, the brewery definitely embraces it.

The company's goal is to offer drinkers a unique experience, but it never seeks new for new's sake. Inspired by forgotten recipes, flavors, and ingredients, every Forbidden Root beer starts with a big idea that embodies a concept. Then, its brewers find the appropriate botanicals and build the beer, layering complexity with subtlety, rather than merely replicating a style. This approach gives Forbidden Root the freedom to step outside the bounds of traditional styles and offer an authentic experience while still respecting best brewing practices.

FIG DUBBEL
BELGIAN-STYLE DUBBEL.

Forbidden Root has a constant influx of new ingredients that it evaluates for flavor and appropriateness in beer. At some point, the brewery became interested in figs and reached out to the California Fig Advisory Board, which presented Forbidden Root with a variety of different figs in a number of different forms. Loving the rich, caramelized fruit flavors, the brewery immediately saw the potential for their use in brewing. Around the same time, its founder, Robert Finkel, had become interested (okay, let's just say obsessed) in fig leaves and got some in to evaluate. Fruit leaves often have some interesting and useful aromas and are a fun and surprising ingredient to use. As it turned out, the brew team found the nutty, woody, and creamy—almost vanilla—notes of the dried fig leaves quite captivating.

Fast-forward a couple of years, and Forbidden Root's head brewer, BJ Pichman, had the idea to combine the two ingredients in a Belgian-style Dubbel. These beers are dark and richly aromatic, with their body typically lightened up by the use of sugar or caramelized sugar. Mission fig syrup played that role beautifully thanks to its high sugar content, which lightened the beer's body while contributing layers of caramelized raisin and fig aromas—not to mention a somewhat creamy mouthfeel. When Forbidden Root brews with unusual ingredients, it always wants to put them into context where they can shine, and that's certainly the case here. The fig leaves add a subtle nutty character that blends nicely with the fruit. Belgian yeast adds another fruity layer, and vanilla overtones add a hint of what might be mistaken as barrel character. A little tannic woodiness closes out the rich-tasting Fig Dubbel.

	Extract	All Grain
Estimated original gravity (OG)	1.069	1.069
Estimated SRM	30	30
Estimated IBU's	18	18
Estimated alcohol ABV %	7.5%	7.5%
Suggested fermentation temperature	70°F	70°F

KIT: EXTRACT

KIT: ALL GRAIN

Specific Recipe Information

Add candi sugar and molasses with 10 minutes left in boil.

At end of the boil, add 2 ounces of fig leaves and whirlpool for 15 minutes.

Near terminal gravity, add 1 pound of Mission Figs (pureed) to fermenter.

Yeast: WLP530

Malt Extracts/Additions

12 pounds Pilsner Extract

Turn burner off before adding. Boil for 60 minutes.

Steeping Grain

1.5 pounds Special B Malt

0.75 pounds Aromatic Malt

0.5 pounds dark candi sugar *

0.5 pounds molasses *

Use a grain bag. Add to water immediately. Remove steeping grain at 170°F.

Hops

1.25 ounces Tettnang

Wort Clarifying Treatment

Whirlfloc (use ½ to 1 Tablet) – Add at last 5 minutes of the boil.

Grain

12 pounds Pilsner Malt

1.5 pounds Special B Malt

0.75 pounds Aromatic Malt

0.5 pound dark candi sugar

0.5 pounds molasses

Turn burner off before adding. Boil for 60 minutes.

Recipe based on: 70% Mash Efficiency

Strike Water Temperature: 161°F

Mash Temperature: 152°F

Time: 60 minutes

Sparge Water Temperature: 170°F

Time: Until KF

Hops

1.25 ounces Tettnang

Boil for 60 minutes

Wort Clarifying Treatment

Whirlfloc (use ½ to 1 Tablet) – Add at last 5 minutes of the boil.

FOUNDATION BREWING COMPANY

PORTLAND MAINE

Beer Name

MASALA
SAISON

Foundation's story began in 2010 when Joel Mahaffey and John Bonney brewed a batch of beer together at a new homebrew shop in Bangor, Maine. Finding common interest and taste, Mahaffey and Bonney developed a friendship around the science and art of brewing, and over the next two years, swapped beers, ideas, recipes, and techniques. While the pair has a love for all beer styles, the level of freedom and diverse ingredients of Belgian beers inspired much of their experiments.

The brewery was founded in 2012 by Joel and Christie Mahaffey and John and Tina Bonney, and opened in February of 2014 at One Industrial Way in Portland, Maine, an address that has become a breeding ground for world-class Maine beers. Initially offering two farmhouse-style beers, Mahaffey and Bonney couldn't suppress their desire to brew different styles for long and released their first non-Belgian beer, Burnside Brown Ale, in the fall of 2014. Once Pandora's box was opened, Foundation began adding other non-Belgian beers to its portfolio and now brews several American- and British-style beers year-round.

Foundation is well known for its Maine IPA, Epiphany, a Double IPA dry hopped with Mosaic, Citra, and Ella hops and designed to showcase the glorious flavor and aromatics of hops without any astringent bitterness. Other popular beers include Afterglow (an American IPA), Zuurzing (a sour farmhouse ale), Burnside (a Brown Ale), Riverton Flyer (a Pilsner), Venture (a Maine IPA), and Forge (a Russian Imperial Stout). Mahaffey and Bonney also have a deep passion for wild fermented beer, and so Foundation filled its first oak barrels in the summer of 2014, released its first wild fermented beer in the fall of 2015, and has steadily increased its barrel program ever since.

Masala is a spiced Saison, which plays off the natural phenolic character produced by Belgian yeasts and is enhanced by a blend of spices commonly used to make masala chai, a sweet, milky tea first popularized in India. After fermentation is complete, Foundation infuses the beer with cinnamon, cardamom, star anise, ginger, black pepper, cloves, nutmeg, orange zest, and vanilla. As a finishing touch, Mahaffey and Bonney also add three teabags of black tea. Since Saisons are often brewed with spices, this combination of flavors works in harmony to create an incredibly enjoyable beer that is surprising in its flavor profile.

	Extract	All Grain
Estimated original gravity (OG)	1.056	1.056
Estimated SRM	3.1	3.1
Estimated IBU's	21	21
Estimated alcohol ABV %	6.8%	6.8%
Suggested fermentation temperature	75°F	75°F

Specific Recipe Information

Adjust 11.25 quarts of water to 200 ppm calcium with gypsum or calcium chloride. Mash per directions. Collect 6.5 gallons total. Boil per directions, with a 20 minute whirlpool at end of the boil. Pitch favorite Saison yeast (Wyeast 3726 is closest to our strain) and ferment completely.

Before packaging, make the tea. Add 6 to 8 inches of cinnamon stick, 8 green cardamom pods, 2 star anise, 2 inches of fresh ginger sliced thiny, half a teaspoon of whole black peppercorns, 10 whole cloves, and 4 ounces of dextrose (exclude if force carbonating) to 5 cups of cold water. Bring to a boil and then remove from heat. Add ½ teaspoon of fresh nutmeg, ½ teaspoon of fresh orange zest, one vanilla bean split, and 2 bags of black tea. Steep for 20 minutes. Pour hot through a sanitized strainer into a bottling bucket or keg. Rack beer on top. Package normally.

KIT: EXTRACT

Malt Extracts/Additions

9.5 pounds Pilsner Liquid Malt Extract

1.25 pounds Vienna Malt

1 pound Flaked Wheat

1 pound Dextrose

0.5 pounds Acidulated Malt

Turn burner off before adding. Boil for 60 minutes.

Steeping Grain

None

Hops

0.25 ounces CTZ First wort

0.25 ounces Crystal added 15 minutes from end of boil

0.25 ounces Saaz added 15 minutes from end of boil

0.75 ounces Crystal added at whirlpool

0.75 ounces Saaz added at whirlpool

Wort Clarifying Treatment

Whirlfloc (use ½ to 1 Tablet) – Add at last 5 minutes of the boil.

KIT: ALL GRAIN

Grain

6.25 pounds Pilsner Malt

1.25 pounds Vienna Malt

1 pound Flaked Wheat

1 pound Dextrose

0.5 pounds Acidulated Malt

Turn burner off before adding. Boil for 75 minutes.

Recipe based on: 70% Mash Efficiency

Strike Water Temperature: 159°F

Mash Temperature: 148°F

Time: 75 minutes

Sparge Water Temperature: 168°F

Hops

0.25 ounces CTZ First wort

0.25 ounces Crystal added 15 minutes from end of boil

0.25 ounces Saaz added 15 minutes from end of boil

0.75 ounces Crystal added at whirlpool

0.75 ounces Saaz added at whirlpool

FOUR QUARTERS BREWING

WINOOSKI VERMONT

FOUR QUARTEREZ

AMERICAN WILD ALE

Four Quarters embodies the cycle of life, the journey that each ingredient makes on its way to your glass: A seed, carefully planted and nurtured, growing with the energy of the sun, Earth, wind, and rain; The fruits harvested, later release their seeds; and the cycle of life starts again. When Four Quarters creates new beers, it's celebrating the Earth and everything that grows within. The company's logo and ethos, the moon phases, encapsulates this cycle, present in every living thing. The hope is that by thoughtfully crafting each and every beer with this cycle in mind, the brewery can pass to its drinkers, not just a glass of delicious brew, but its passion, its love, and its thankfulness, for all things in the natural world.

Operating in Winooski Vermont, Four Quarters Brewing is inspired by traditional Belgian and American approaches to crafting beers. It strives to push the creative envelope with off-the-wall concoctions that incorporate locally sourced ingredients, mixed fermentation, and barrel aging.

At the heart of these crazy ferments is a farm fresh cocktail-inspired lineup that includes: Little Umbrellas (a Piña Colada inspired rum barrel-aged sour ale conditioned on toasted coconut and pineapples), Moscow Mule (a gin barrel-aged Saison brewed with lime zest, juice, and fresh ginger), Pickleback (a bourbon barrel-aged saison conditioned on honeydew, cucumbers, and dill), Tomato Basil Fleur de Lis (an oak barrel-aged tart saison conditioned on roasted tomatoes, fresh basil, fresh grated horseradish, celery puree, and Tabasco peppers), and Whiskey Sour (a Witbier with sweet and bitter orange peel, mixed fermentation in bourbon barrels and conditioned on sour cherries).

Four Quarterez (pronounced "core-TARE-ez") was the first in the brewery's line of cocktail-inspired beers. It started, as so many good things do, with a happy accident—a misprinted hooded sweatshirt. Every fall, Four Quarters plays host to an all-day event dedicated to the beauty of cask ales. In its first year, new hoodies were ordered for staff members, and after their arrival, an odd spelling of Quarters was discovered. The brewery had been given a Spanish flair: "Quarteres" with an extra "e." As a result, "Four Quarterez!" was sounded all weekend, inspiring the creation of a mojito beer with the same name for the next Cinco de Mayo.

Seeing Emeril Lagasse make an ugli fruit mojito initially presented an opportunity for an even more original recipe. But ugli fruit, a Jamaican tangelo, proved to be a bit too sour, without enough of a balanced degree of sweetness, so Four Quarters opted for orange zest and juice to compensate. Grapefruit is another option for those who want to create a more sour final product. The result will be the same—a delectable, thirst quenching, multi-sensory experience that cleanses the palate, making the drinker want to come back for more. This ale has beautiful fresh mint aromatics, a nice medium-bodied mouthfeel with a balance of ripened citrus sweetness, followed by a tart exclamation point.

	Extract	All Grain
Estimated original gravity (OG)	1.044–1.046	1.044–1.046
Estimated SRM	5.0–5.5	5.0–5.5
Estimated IBU's	7.0–7.5	7.0–7.5
Estimated alcohol ABV %	4.5–4.7%	4.5–4.7%
Suggested fermentation temperature	70 to 72°F	70 to 72°F

Specific Recipe Information

Heat water enough to dissolve DME, remove from heat and let cool to 120°F. Throw in a handful of crushed base grain in a muslin bag, flush with CO_2, and cover with kettle lid. Keep wort temperature between 100 and 120°F for the next 24 to 48 hours. You can maintain the temperature either by keeping in an oven with the light on or by warming on your burner every so often. Taste the wort at 24 hours and every 4 to 6 hours to determine the proper amount of sour you desire (or 3.4 pH). When sourness is reached, remove the grains, add in the steeping grains in a muslin bag, and start heating your wort. Remove steeping grains at 165°F. Add hops at boil and boil for 10 minutes. Low bitterness is desired, so you don't need to boil for a full 60 minutes. After 10 minutes, chill to 70°F, rack to carboy or bucket, and pitch your favorite saison yeast.

After primary fermentation is complete, transfer to secondary on top of ¼ ounce of orange zest, ½ quart of orange juice, and a ½ ounce of spearmint leaves. Taste after two days and proceed when you think it's ready!

KIT: EXTRACT

Malt Extracts/Additions

3 pounds Wheat DME

2 pounds Extra Light DME

Steeping Grain

4 ounces Caramel/Crystal 40 L

Use a grain bag. Add to water immediately. Remove steeping grain at 170°F.

Hops

1 ounce Hallertauer

Bittering Hops are boiled for 10 minutes.

KIT: ALL GRAIN

Grain

4 pounds 2-Row Pale Malt

4 pound Flaked Wheat

8 ounces Caramel/Crystal 40 L

Recipe based on: 70% Mash Efficiency

Strike Water Temperature: 162°F

Mash Temperature: 147°F

Time: 60 minutes

Sparge Water Temperature: 168°F

Time: 30 minutes

Hops

1 ounce Hallertauer

Bittering hops are boiled for 60 minutes.

Secondary

½ ounce spearmint leaves

¼ ounce orange zest

1 quart orange juice

FREE WILL BREWING COMPANY

PERKASIE PENNSYLVANIA

SAFEWORD
DOUBLE IPA

Free Will began as so many other breweries have started: as a romantic story of two longtime friends, John Stemler and Dominic Capece, who were amateur brewers just making what they wanted for themselves. And then, somehow, it grew into something more. Stemler went to school for biology and chemistry at Ursinus College, but didn't get into brewing until 2008. Brewing as a team, the two started getting noticed by some industry professionals through a local homebrew store association and were encouraged to take it to the next level. After two years of planning, building, and lots of paperwork, Free Will sold its first beer in January of 2012. Since then, the original 8,600 square foot (799 square meter) facility and 7.5-barrel system have grown into a 38,000 square foot (3,530 square meter) space and a fifteen-barrel brewhouse with sixty-barrel fermenters. The main facility brews and bottles several brands, with distribution in the Northeast, as well as Belgium. In addition, the Sour Cellar currently houses over 1,100 barrels of sour beer to be shared with an ever-expanding market of sour beer lovers.

To the founders, Free Will means many things. It embodies Stemler's brewing style, in that he enjoys drinking and brewing all styles. Nothing seems out of reach when you consider that the boundaries of the brewing industry are only constrained by the possibilities of science and imagination. Free Will is also easy to remember and the word "free" is one of the most powerful words in the English language.

The main facility's taproom is open seven days a week and has food trucks on the weekends as well as several events per month, including a Sour Sunday that draws patrons from far and wide. In the coming year, several other taprooms are slated to open regionally to help spread the word of Free Will. Further expansion plans include partnering with a broad spectrum of wholesalers that can carry the brewery's products farther and wider, both nationally and internationally, as well as continuing to bring good beer to good people using their own "Free Will."

Safeword was originally formulated as a collaboration for Philly Beer Week 2014 with a friend who is a brewer and owner at another Pennsylvania brewery. The idea to create such a radical and aggressive beer was born out of a desire to make something completely out of left field that still manages to remain balanced. It had to hurt just enough to warrant the name "Safeword." The first test batch was murky, sweet, and hot as hell. And even though the sweet and the heat achieved balance, Stemler felt that it might be a bit too radical. When Safeword debuted at a festival in March of 2014, however, the non-stop line, repeat servings, and excited buzz among the 3,000 festival goers solidified the level of intensity that this beer needed to have.

The first thirty-barrel batch was produced for its intended week of craziness and people lost their minds. It sold out quickly. Mango up front, heat in the back, and a cult following of sadistic fans. To this day Safeword is Free Will's most requested beer via email and direct messaging. After a few more batches it was clear that Safeword was here to stay. But where do you put a beer like that in such a large portfolio? The answer was clear. Free Will didn't have a "stupid holiday beer." So although Safeword is the antithesis of traditional holiday spiced ales, it's now released around the holidays on draft and in limited bottles.

	Extract	All Grain
Estimated original gravity (OG)	1.100–1.105	None Provided
Estimated SRM	8	
Estimated IBU's	105–115	
Estimated alcohol ABV %	10.2%	
Suggested fermentation temperature	66°F	

Specific Recipe Information

Hopping schedule: 1 ounce of Apollo at 60 minutes, 1 ounce of Chinook and 1 ounce of Simcoe at 15 minutes, 1 ounce of Apollo at 10 minutes, and 1 ounce of Simcoe at 5 minutes. Ferment with super-clean, strong American yeast strain such as White Labs San Diego Super Yeast or similar. When fermentation slows, add 1 to 2 pounds aseptic mango puree to fermentor. Wait for fermentation to complete before adding dry hops. Dry hop for 5 days post fermentation: 2 ounces Citra, 2 ounces Simcoe, and 2 ounces Chinook. Add 2 habaneros (pureed) to dry hop pouch.

KIT: EXTRACT

Malt Extracts/Additions

6.6 pounds Vienna LME	
6.0 pounds Pale Ale DME	
1.0 pound Wheat DME	
1.0 pound Dextrose	

Turn burner off before adding. Boil for 60 minutes.

Steeping Grain

2 ounces Acidulated Malt

Use a grain bag. Add to water immediately. Remove steeping grain at 170°F.

Hops

2 ounces Apollo 18.3%	
3 ounces Chinook 11.2%	
4 ounces Simcoe 14.1%	
2 ounces Citra 14.2%	

Bittering hops are boiled for 60 minutes.

Flavoring hops are boiled for 15, 10, and 5 minutes.

Dry hops for 5 days

Wort Clarifying Treatment

Whirlfloc (use ½ to 1 Tablet) – Add at last 5 minutes of the boil.

KIT: ALL GRAIN

Grain

8.5 pounds Vienna	
8.5 pounds Pale	
1.5 pounds Wheat	
2 ounces Acidulated Malt	
1.0 pound Dextrose (add at flameout)	
Recipe based on: 70% mash efficiency	
Strike Water Temperature: 170°F with a grain temp of 70°F	
Mash Temperature: 158°F	
Time: 60 minutes	
Sparge Water Temperature: 170°F	
Time: Until full kettle volume	

Hops

2 ounces Apollo 18.3%	
3 ounces Chinook 11.2%	
4 ounces Simcoe 14.1%	
2 ounces Citra 14.2%	

Bittering hops are boiled for 60 minutes.

Flavoring hops are boiled for 15, 10, and 5 minutes.

Dry hops for 5 days.

Wort Clarifying Treatment

Whirlfloc (use ½ to 1 Tablet) – Add at last 5 minutes of the boil.

FUNKY BUDDHA BREWERY

OAKLAND PARK FLORIDA

FIRE IN THE HOLE

FRUIT/ VEGETABLE BEER

Funky Buddha Brewery's history began in 2007 when owner Ryan Sentz transformed the diminutive R & R Tea Bar in Boca Raton into a loungey, Buddha-themed hangout serving some of the finest craft brewed beers available—a rarity in South Florida at the time. As the popularity of Sentz's new beer hangout grew, he decided to incorporate his passion for homebrewing. Utilizing a one-barrel brewhouse—barely larger than most homebrew setups—Funky Buddha began producing culinary-inspired beers made with whole, natural ingredients from Florida and beyond.

The first batches were an instant hit. Beers like Rum-Barrel Aged Red Ale, Orange-Creamsicle Wheat, and Ginger Lemongrass attracted folks looking to try something new. A few months later, Sentz created the beer that broke the mold: Maple Bacon Coffee Porter. This rich beer had it all: smoky and salty bacon, rich and sweet maple syrup, and roasty coffee. It was breakfast in a glass. It also tapped perfectly into the craft brewing renaissance sweeping beer-reviewing websites like BeerAdvocate at the time. With a small initial bottle release, Maple Bacon Coffee Porter was traded across the country and internationally by beer lovers as far away as New York, California, and Denmark, who commented on the intense flavors Funky Buddha had managed to blend into a balanced brew.

Almost overnight, Maple Bacon Coffee Porter became the top rated porter on BeerAdvocate—an impressive feat for a brewpub less than one year old (it has since won a gold medal in the 2016 World Beer Cup). With the demand for Funky Buddha's beers skyrocketing, Sentz got together with his brother KC, a former engineer for Motorola, and started to work on what would become Funky Buddha Brewery in Oakland Park, Florida.

Since opening in June 2013, Funky Buddha has grown to become one of the largest breweries in Florida. Sentz and company continue to brew according to the mantra of bold flavored beers made exactingly with natural ingredients. Beers like Last Snow Coconut and Coffee Porter, French Toast Double Brown, The Love Below (a barrel-aged Russian Imperial stout with cherries and chocolate), and dozens more have become sought after nationwide. Its annual Maple Bacon Coffee Porter Festival and bottle release is held every January at the brewery, and its expansive taproom hosts hundreds of events, bottle releases, and beer pairings each year, making it a destination for locals and tourists alike.

The Funky Buddha approach to brewing is simple: stay true to flavor. It does that by using high quality, real ingredients, whether that's whole fruit, juice, spices, coffee, cacao nibs, or the like, even if it means a more expensive product. Funky Buddha isn't subtle with its flavors, either. If it's going to be a blood orange IPA, this brewery wants you to get the same kind of bright, fresh citrus flavor as if you were biting straight into a piece of fruit. Even so, Funky Buddha always strives for balance—it has to be a beer at the end of the day. Finally, we have fun—we try to recall flavor memories or experiences and build on them. When you taste No Crusts, the idea is to get people to remember what it was like to eat one of your mom's peanut butter-and-jelly sandwiches with the crusts cut off.

In choosing to showcase Fire in the Hole, Funky Buddha wanted to pick a beer that speaks to a bit of its South Florida heritage. Starting with a classic English red ale, this beer incorporates whole Habanero chili peppers, which impart the kind of fantastic fruitiness you find in island cuisine. On their own, the heat of the peppers would be a little intense, so the brewery also uses juicy red raspberries to temper that spice and add some sweetness. The result is a pepper beer, but one that is also very drinkable.

	Extract	All Grain
Estimated original gravity (OG)	None Provided	None Provided
Estimated SRM		
Estimated IBU's		
Estimated alcohol ABV %		
Suggested fermentation temperature		

Specific Recipe Information

Ferment with California Ale yeast at 70°F. Add 4 pounds of raspberries to secondary for 1 week. Add 1 ounce of habanero to secondary for 1 week.

KIT: EXTRACT

Malt Extracts/Additions

5 pounds Pilsner Malt Extract

4.5 pounds Pale Malt Extract

Steeping Grain

1 pound Honey Malt

12 ounces Caramel 120L

12 ounces White Wheat

1.4 ounces Roasted Barley

Use a grain bag. Add to water immediately. Remove steeping grain at 170°F.

Hops

0.5 ounces Nugget

1 ounce Tettnang

Bittering hops are boiled for 60 minutes.

Bittering/flavor hops are boiled for 30 minutes.

Wort Clarifying Treatment

KICK Carageenan (1 Tablet) – Add at last 5 minutes of the boil.

Bottling

4 ounces corn sugar – Boil with 2 cups of water for 5 minutes.

KIT: ALL GRAIN

Grain

None Provided

KANE BREWING COMPANY

OCEAN
NEW JERSEY

MALUS
BELGIAN STRONG DARK ALE

The idea for Kane Brewing Company started during a trip across Europe, where founder Michael Kane was exposed to full-bodied English ales, crisp authentic German lagers, refreshing Weiss beers, and an array of unique Belgian ales. Following his return, he looked to some of the small, recently opened craft breweries of New England as a way to explore new styles and flavors in beer. It was during one of these visits to a small Vermont brewery where he learned about homebrewing. Kane brewed his first batch, a German wheat beer, during his senior year in college and decided before it finished fermenting that he was going to open a brewery someday. Years later, he realized his dream when he started Kane Brewing Company in Ocean, New Jersey.

Kane Brewing Company opened its doors in 2011 with a focus on creating hop-forward American- and Belgian-influenced ales. At the core of its lineup is Head High, an American-style IPA that has quickly become a staple on the draft lists of local bars and restaurants. The passion for brewing hop-forward beers and the success of Head High afforded the brewery the opportunity to branch out and experiment with innovative styles and creative uses of new ingredients.

Over the last six years, Kane has made its mark with its barrel-aging program, using various bourbon, cognac, rum, and wine barrels to enhance flavor profiles and create distinctive one-of-a-kind beers. This can take extreme patience, though, as flavor development might persist for several months or years. The brewery also continually looks to source ingredients such as honey, coffee, and apple cider from local suppliers in the area. Inventive uses of these ingredients and well-planned twists on classic styles have led to exciting, high-quality, award-winning ales.

Kane Brewing Company is poised to continue its growth with its expanded square footage and fermentation capacity, along with a recently added multiple-format, in-house packaging operation. At the heart of Kane Brewing Company's philosophy is a focus on consistently crafting the highest quality beers, while striving for steady improvement through growth. Self-distributing and maintaining a complete focus on its home state of New Jersey allows the brewery to ensure the highest level of both beer freshness and service responsiveness while keeping in close contact with its growing number of loyal customers.

Malus was originally conceived to celebrate Kane's inaugural bottling run during its first year of production. The idea to incorporate local seasonal ingredients was certainly not new at the time, but brewing a dark Belgian beer with apple cider from a nearby orchard in lieu of Belgian candi sugar was novel in 2011. Starting with a fairly traditional malt bill for a Belgian-style Strong Dark Ale, hundreds of gallons of freshly pressed, unpasteurized, local cider are then added to the kettle.

The cider is boiled to create a reduction that mimics the use of Belgian candi sugar with a slightly different flavor contribution. Instead of dark fruit and raisins, the reduced apple cider adds a caramelized, candy-apple flavor to the beer. Post fermentation, Kane adds fresh orange zest, cinnamon, allspice, clove, and nutmeg for a mulled cider effect that keeps this beer seasonally appropriate from the first chilly days of autumn right up through the holidays. The result is a big, full-bodied, traditionally inspired but locally redefined Belgian-style ale suitable for drinking by itself, with a festive holiday meal, or in the company of family at a seasonal gathering.

	Extract	All Grain
Estimated original gravity (OG)	21 plato	21 plato
Estimated SRM		
Estimated IBU's	19.5	19.5
Estimated alcohol ABV %	9.7%	9.7%
Suggested fermentation temperature	Pitch at 64°F; rise to 68°F	Pitch at 64°F; rise to 68°F

Specific Recipe Information

1.35 gallons of unpasteurized local apple cider. Add the cider to the kettle and boil for 15 to 20 minutes to reduce. Then add water and Liquid Malt Extract and bring to a boil.

Make a tea with warm, de-aerated water and add to secondary. Adjust spicing to taste.

KIT: EXTRACT

Malt Extracts/Additions

11 pounds Light Liquid Malt Extract

1.0 pound Liquid Wheat Extract

Turn burner off before adding. Boil for 90 minutes.

Steeping Grain

1.5 pounds Special B Malt

0.5 pound Biscuit Malt

Use a grain bag. Add to water immediately. Remove steeping grain at 170°F.

Hops

90 minutes: 0.25 ounce Columbus @ 15AA

Spices:

3 grams cinnamon

0.25 grams clove, allspice, and nutmeg

Zest from 5 large oranges

KIT: ALL GRAIN

Grain

16 pounds European Pilsner

1.5 pounds Special B Malt

0.5 pounds Biscuit Malt

0.5 pound White Wheat

Turn burner off before adding. Boil for 90 minutes.

Recipe based on:
70% Mash Efficiency

Strike Water Temperature: 162°F

Mash Temperature: 150°F

Time: 60 minutes.

Sparge Water Temperature: 178°F

Time: 75 minutes.

Hops

90 minutes: 0.25 ounce Columbus @ 15AA

Spices:

3 grams cinnamon

0.25 grams clove, allspice and nutmeg

Zest from 5 large oranges

KENT FALLS BREWING COMPANY

**KENT
CONNECTICUT**

COFFEEMAKER
COFFEE BRETT IPA

Although Kent Falls was established to further the farmhouse brewing model in Connecticut, a state without any farmhouse breweries or hop farms at the time of the company's inception, the goal was never to limit the brewing exclusively to traditional farmhouse-style beers. The inspiration was the ethos of farmhouse brewing: rural brewing tied to a place, its resources, and especially, refreshment. Or, in other words: simple, expressive, and highly drinkable beers. However basic or experimental, Kent Falls strives to make beers that a farmer or a brewer would find satisfaction in after a long day's work. Beers that could, hopefully, bridge the gap between the extreme beer enthusiast and the casual drinker merely seeking something approachable. Kent Falls operates under the belief that extreme beer can often be deceptively simple (and even low-ABV). It can derive flavor from a handful of distinctive ingredients, used precisely and to underline existing flavors, or as the result of a unique fermentation process.

In its first year of operation, Kent Falls released almost fifty different beers, eschewing flagships and year-round core brands in favor of seasonality and variety. Many beers are brewed only once or twice a year, while seasonal regulars like Waymaker Brett IPA often serve as the jumping-off point for further experimentation. A tropical, light Brett IPA serves as an excellent base for a touch of citrusy coffee character or an enhanced tropical profile with the addition of exotic fruits. Other beers, like Walking Away in Slow Motion as the Car Explodes Behind You, a fruited Imperial Gose, are a challenge to achieve subtlety and nuance while taking on an over-the-top recipe concept.

As Kent Falls grows, it is expanding its barrel program, its range of fruited sours, aged farmhouse beer, and other mixed-culture experiments. At the same time, its goal is to treat even the simplest styles and most approachable beers as an avenue for experimentation and refinement.

Coffeemaker is a Brett IPA made with coffee that uses the brewery's Waymaker Brett IPA as a foundation. Waymaker was the second beer conceived for the Kent Falls lineup and one of the few beers that it releases several times throughout the year. To demonstrate the flexibility of *Brettanomyces* yeast and the many flavors that can be paired with it, the brewery expanded its lineup with coffee, fruit, imperial, and other variations on Brett IPA. The addition of coffee from Irving Farm, a roaster nearby in the Hudson Valley, creates a highly unique experience. The Brett IPA underneath is dry, pale, and light, while the coffee enhances the perception of maltiness, fruit, and citrus aromatics.

Most coffee beers combine the dark roast qualities of a porter or stout with that of the coffee itself, but Coffeemaker deals with complementary rather than overlapping flavor profiles. A variety of roasts can be used with success. Before brewing each batch, the Kent Falls brewery staff and the Irving Farm roastery staff meet for a cupping and an experimental blending session, determining the coffee and quantity to be used in the next beer. Due to the oxygen-scavenging qualities of Brett yeast, Coffeemaker ages surprisingly well, retaining its nuanced coffee characteristics for months after packaging, while slowly aging into a unique wild beer.

	Extract	All Grain
Estimated original gravity (OG)	1.055	1.053
Estimated SRM	4	4
Estimated IBU's	32	32
Estimated alcohol ABV %	5.6%	5.6%
Suggested fermentation temperature	74°F	74°F

Specific Recipe Information

Dry hop for four days and then prepare beer for packaging. In keg or bottling bucket, add 32 ounces of double-strength coffee (brewed hot and then cooled to room temperature) to beer. Bottle or keg as usual.

KIT: EXTRACT

Malt Extracts/Additions

7.5 pounds Extra Light Extract

4 ounces Maltodextrine

Turn burner off before adding. Boil for 60 minutes.

Steeping Grain

None

Hops

0.5 ounces Glacier – Bittering

1.5 ounces Glacier – Whirlpool

1 ounce Centennial – Whirlpool

2 ounces Centenial – Dry Hop

1 ounce Chinook – Dry Hop

Wort Clarifying Treatment

Whirlfloc (use ½ to 1 Tablet) – Add at last 5 minutes of the boil.

KIT: ALL GRAIN

Grain

8 pounds 2-Row

2 pounds White Wheat Malt

Recipe based on: 70% Mash Efficiency

Hops

0.5 ounces Glacier – Bittering

1.5 ounce Glacier – Whirlpool

1 ounce Centennial – Whirlpool

2 ounce Centenial – Dry Hop

1 ounce Chinook – Dry Hop

Wort Clarifying Treatment

Whirlfloc (use ½ to 1 Tablet) – Add at last 5 minutes of the boil.

THE LOST ABBEY

SAN MARCOS CALIFORNIA

Beer Name

PÊCHE DE TOMME

AMERICAN WILD ALE

Port Brewing and The Lost Abbey were founded in San Marcos, California, (a suburb of San Diego) in 2006. One of the most noteworthy aspects of the brewery was that its founders launched it with the ambitious plan of producing two distinctly separate lines of beers made in the same facility. From the beginning, the goal was to make West Coast-style beers and brand them under the Port Brewing name, while simultaneously producing a Belgian-inspired line of beers branded under The Lost Abbey.

Both brands have been made continuously since their debut in 2006. In 2015, a third brand, The Hop Concept, was created for the release of a set of IPAs designed with maximum flavor and aroma in mind. With eight beers now in the portfolio, The Hop Concept and its Hop Freshener IPAs exist to explore new hop combinations and dry hopping techniques.

All told, the three brands of vibrant, bold, and flavor-forward beers represent over fifty unique releases each year. In short, fans of the brewery have an incredible spectrum of flavors to choose from when it comes to the variety of beers produced in San Marcos. Some of the most sought-after and interesting explorations involve experimental beers and the use of oak barrels for aging and the creation of both sour and non-sour, spirit-aged libations. Port Brewing and The Lost Abbey started out with 100 oak barrels in their barrel program in 2006. Today, the company's collection includes some 1,300 oak barrels along with two 110-barrel foeders (upright oak tanks). And it won't stop there.

The Lost Abbey is well known for producing a beer known simply as Cuvee de Tomme each year. Named after cofounder Tomme Arthur, this landmark beer is a blend of a strong ale brewed with raisins that's aged in used oak barrels with sour cherries and wild yeast cultures. As complex as a red wine, the time spent in oak provides numerous tannic backbones in addition to the structure to age this beer for years.

One day, the brewers thought it would be fun to reimagine this beer with peaches instead of sour cherries. In order to keep the balance in spec though, The Lost Abbey lightened the grain bill, replacing some of the darker crystal malts with brighter biscuit malt and even some spicy rye malt. While the commercial beer is aged in a mixture of brandy, bourbon, and red wine oak barrels, this brew at home can be aged on medium-toasted oak spirals to achieve a similar texture. Most notably, the beer will benefit from the light oak notes and some vanillin contributions.

The recipe was designed with some acidity in mind (from a wild secondary fermentation). And it should be noted that it's possible the peaches will bring their own microflora to the brew. If fidelity to The Lost Abbey recipe is the goal, feel free to pitch the dregs from two or three of your favorite sour beers and let the brewing gods do their thing.

	Extract	All Grain
Estimated original gravity (OG)		None Provided
Estimated SRM		
Estimated IBU's		
Estimated alcohol ABV %		
Suggested fermentation temperature	68°F	

KIT: EXTRACT

Specific Recipe Information

A simple two-week primary fermentation followed by nine to twelve months on peaches should yield an amazing brew. The Lost Abbey brewers love the fresh peaches from California's Masumoto Farms for their brews. Each June and July they receive about 600 pounds of peaches and nectarines from this grower. Of course, any organic stone fruit will work—including frozen ones. They recommend a ratio of ¾ to 1 pound of fruit per gallon of beer.

Once primary fermentation has completed, cold condition beer to remove yeast and trub. Transfer to carboy or small oak barrel. Add peaches to receiving vessel. If glass or stainless, add oak spirals. If using cultures to acidify the beer, drink up and harvest into vessel for aging.

Malt Extracts/Additions

7.5 pounds Pale Liquid Malt Extract

7 pounds corn sugar

Steeping Grain

1 pound Rye Malt

1 pound Honey Malt

12 ounces Caramel Wheat Malt

8 ounces Caramel 40 L

Use a grain bag. Add to water immediately. Remove steeping grain at 170°F.

Hops

1.25 ounces Magnum

Bittering hops are boiled for 60 minutes.

Wort Clarifying Treatment:

Whirlfloc (1 Tablet) – Add at last 5 minutes of the boil.

Bottling

4 ounces corn sugar – Boil with 2 cups of water for 5 minutes.

NEWBURGH BREWING COMPANY

NEWBURGH NEW YORK

Beer Name

C.A.F.E. SOUR

FRUIT/ VEGETABLE BEER

Christopher Basso, Charlie Benedetti, and Paul Halayko founded Newburgh Brewing Company in 2012, but the story begins with Basso and his professional beginnings as a brewer at the Brooklyn Brewery. After brewing as part of the team at Brooklyn for nearly seven years, he decided he wanted to branch out on his own and to do so where he grew up: in New York State's Hudson Valley.

Basso quickly decided that the City of Newburgh was a fitting place for a brewery. While it may not have the greatest reputation, Newburgh is a city with great beauty, a rich history, and an energetic population working hard to change its reputation. Basso knew that a brewery named for the city itself could help with the overall renaissance of Newburgh. After much searching, he finally found the brewery's home: a 160-year-old brick warehouse next to the Hudson River. Soon after, Basso enlisted the help of his lifelong childhood friend, Paul Halayko, who then brought on his uncle, Charlie Benedetti. The building had been located, the team was formed, and the brewery was born.

Since first brewing its flagship Newburgh Cream Ale in 2012, Newburgh Brewing has made over forty-five styles of beer. With six year-round offerings alongside a selection of seasonals and specialty one-offs, the brewery's portfolio ranges from the traditional to the experimental. Newburgh prides itself on the diversity of its offerings, which cover a breadth of styles: some original to great brewing nations like Germany, England, and Belgium and others that honor the audacious and adventurous nature of American craft brewers. The company's gorgeous taproom overlooking the Hudson River has also helped Newburgh become a community gathering place for the Hudson Valley and has established it as part of the fabric of the region. Plus, ever-increasing production and expanding distribution means that with each delicious pint of Newburgh beer raised, the perception and reputation of the City of Newburgh improves a little bit more, too.

In a beer world populated with coffee stouts, coffee porters, and coffee brown ales, Newburgh decided to think outside the box when it came time to brew a coffee beer of its own. C.A.F.E. Sour is an Ethiopian-inspired sour beer with cold-brewed Yirgacheffe coffee. The base beer is kettle soured with Newburgh's house culture of *Lactobacillus*, and it's brewed with two ingredients that are indigenous to Ethiopia: teff and gesho. Teff is a staple grain in the Ethiopian diet—extremely important to Ethiopians both because it can grow in many areas where other crops cannot and because it leads all grains in calcium content. Gesho is an Ethiopian root that contributes distinctive flavors and mild bitterness to C.A.F.E. Sour. Both teff and gesho can be obtained at specialty food stores.

Once fermentation is complete, a cold brew concentrate of locally roasted Yirgacheffe coffee is blended into the finished beer. Due to its popularity, Yirgacheffe should be easy to find. What's the result? A true challenge to your senses. C.A.F.E Sour is far lighter in body and color than your traditional coffee beer, while still possessing a beautiful coffee aroma. And its tartness is a delightful surprise following the rich, roasty aroma, blending perfectly with the acidity of the coffee. In other words, C.A.F.E. Sour is not your average cup of coffee. It's like an alcoholic glass of tart iced coffee that you'll want to drink over and over again.

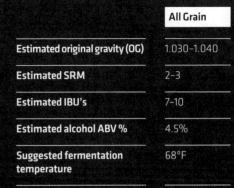

	All Grain
Estimated original gravity (OG)	1.030–1.040
Estimated SRM	2–3
Estimated IBU's	7–10
Estimated alcohol ABV %	4.5%
Suggested fermentation temperature	68°F

Specific Recipe Information

Boil the Teff in 1 gallon of water for 30 minutes. Add enough cold water (measure it) to bring to 149°F and mash in remaining grains. Mash at 149°F for 90 mintutes, raise to 156°F and mash 30 minutes. Bring mash to 170°F and sparge to bring kettle volume to 5.5 gallons. Bring wort in kettle to 180°F and then cool to 110°F. Inoculate with Lactobacillus and try to maintain 110°F for 24 hours (check pH, should get to around 3.2 pH). Bring wort to boil, add sugar as well as Gesho powder and Hops, and boil for 60 minutes. During whirlpool and cooling, steep sticks in a mesh bag. Ferment at 70°F with a neutral ale yeast. After primary fermentation, make a Yirgacheffe Coffee cold brew concentrate (2 L H2O with .25 lbs Coffee overnight). Strain it and add that to your racked beer before you prime and bottle.

KIT: ALL GRAIN

Grain

3 pounds Whole Grain Teff

4.5 pounds Pale Malt

0.5 pounds Acidulated Malt

1 pound Flaked Oats

0.75 pounds Demerara Sugar
Turn burner off before adding. Boil for 60 minutes.

Recipe based on:
70% Mash Efficiency

Cereal Mash Teff:
Bring to boil for 30 minutes .

Add Cold Water to bring to 149°F and Mash in remaining grains.

Mash Temperature: 149°F

Time: 90 minutes

156°F

Time: 30 minutes

Sparge Water Temperature: 170°F

Hops

5 Gesho Sticks

1.25 pounds Coarse Ground Yirgacheffe Coffee

3 ounces Gesho Powder

2 ounces Hallertauer Hersbrucker @ 2.8% AA

Wort Clarifying Treatment

Whirlfloc (use ½ to 1 Tablet) – Add at last 5 minutes of the boil.

CHARLIE PAPAZIAN

FOUNDER AND PAST PRESIDENT OF THE BREWERS ASSOCIATION

BOULDER COLORADO

The American Homebrewers Association (AHA) was founded in Boulder, Colorado, by engineer and avid homebrewer Charlie Papazian. From its humble beginnings in 1978, the organization has grown to over 46,000 members. Advocates for homebrewers' rights in the United States, the AHA is governed by a committee of homebrewers elected by its members and hosts the world's largest beer competition. The organization also publishes *Zymurgy* magazine and hosts multiple events promoting home beer, cider, and mead making. It's a division of the Brewers Association, a not-for-profit trade association that Papazian founded as the Association of Brewers. Today, it remains dedicated to promoting and protecting amateur and professional craft brewers.

Some of Papazian's other accomplishments include creating the Great American Beer Festival and the World Beer Cup and authoring five bestselling books on beer and brewing. He published his first book, *The Complete Joy of Homebrewing*, in 1984. It has gone on to sell more than 1 million copies and is now in its fourth edition.

Papazian often says that he loves to brew and still enjoys homebrewing because the beer is his own and it's fresh. Well, that's only part of the reason. By adding creativity, twists, turns, and nuances to both extreme and traditional styles of ales and lagers, Papazian's beers are ultimately distinctive and unlike those available at a brewpub or anywhere else. His beers may be aligned with certain beer styles, but there are nuances that provide personalized uniqueness to suit his own tastes perfectly. And when he swings and misses, he has friends that enjoy those beers more than he does. So, it always works out, and he never runs out of the beer he enjoys the most.

GOAT SCROTUM ALE

AMERICAN PORTER

Goat Scrotum Ale has been one of the more popular homebrew recipes from *The Complete Joy of Homebrewing*. It's a dark ale with options to throw in ingredients from the kitchen and the garden. It was first brewed in the mid-1970s, a time when Americans were discovering and beginning to enjoy homebrewing. The name actually comes from the cheesecloth bag that held the crystal malt and other ingredients. It was brewed during one of Papazian's homebrew classes and everyone got into the spirit of making the beer by taking turns massaging and squeezing the warm bag of grains suspended over the kettle.

The recipe itself was inspired not by the spirit of anything goes, but rather anything goes that tastes good. So, the combination of ingredients seemed like a delicious concoction for a beer.

Recipes are guidelines. Guidelines provide the foundation for knowledge and the way ahead for creative digression. That's how Papazian approaches brewing. When he tastes a beer and wants to brew it, his first step is to formulate a hypothetical recipe. Then, there's the contemplative stage of the process. A day, a week, or a month may pass before Papazian revisits his developmental ideas, integrates his enjoyable taste experiences, and proceeds to "goose" the recipe even more. He uses creative options to personalize his beer and encourages others to do the same with Goat Scrotum Ale.

Specific Recipe Information

First of all, pop a homebrew and dissolve your anxieties.

Next, add the crushed grain malt to 2 gallons of water and let steep at 150 to 160°F for 30 minutes. Then remove the grains with a strainer. Add the malt extract, boiling hops, and all of the other ingredients except the finishing hops, yeast, and bottling sugar and boil for 60 minutes. Add Irish moss for the last 10 minutes of the boil. Add the finishing hops for the last 2 minutes of the boil. Strain, sparge, and transfer immediately to 2 gallons of cold water in the fermenter. Top off with additional water to make 5 gallons. Add the yeast when cool and ferment to completion. Bottle when fermentation is complete.

Have another homebrew. When ready, chill, serve, close your eyes, and slip back into the eighteenth century. It is a good porter! And you have a good life.

KIT: EXTRACT

Malt Extracts/Additions

5 pounds of Dark Malt Extract

Steeping Grain

1 pound Caramel 10 L

4 ounces Special B Malt

4 ounces Chocolate Rye Malt

4 ounces Roasted Barley

Grain bag optional

Hops

1.5 ounces Bittering hop of your choice

0.25 ounces Aroma hop of your choice

0.5 pounds Rapadura or 240 ml Blackstrap molasses

1 to 10 small fresh or dried hot chili peppers

6 ounces unsweetened baker's chocolate

60 ml coriander seeds (slightly crushed)

60 ml juniper seeds (slightly crushed)

2 ounces dried orange peel

0.25 teaspoons powdered Irish moss

Bittering hops are boiled for 60 minutes.

Aroma/flavor hops are boiled for 2 minutes.

THE POST BREWING COMPANY

LAFAYETTE COLORADO

The Post Brewing Company was founded in January 2014 in the sleepy town of Lafayette, Colorado. As a rule, Post approaches brewing holistically, which means it takes into account the full experience of enjoying Post beer. Its goal is to deliver a satisfying experience of food, drink, and place that is both fun and memorable, whether it's a fried chicken plate paired with Townie IPA or a hot mess of shrimp washed down with Meathooks Mild Ale. From the All-American Pilsener to the Baltic Porter, Post beers are thoroughly food-minded and are inspired by everything around us. Overall, the approach this brewery takes to making beer draws from personal memories and world experiences to elicit a comforting feeling of familiarity, gentle surprise, and neverending wonder.

Beer Name

BULKY OXEN
ENGLISH-STYLE BARLEYWINE

The Post Brewing Company loves its friends. Even more, it loves making stuff with its friends. So, for its inaugural "Brewing With Friends" beer, brewmaster Bryan Selders asked his old friend Sam Calagione, founder and president of Dogfish Head in Delaware, to brew with him. During a top-secret mandate over a few cocktails, the two hatched the idea for Bulky Oxen.

The name Bulky Oxen was inspired by Babe the Big Blue Ox from the Paul Bunyan fable, a character woven into the Dogfish Head ethos from the beginning. It seemed fitting as Babe was always the trusty companion to Paul Bunyan, and Calagione and Selders have had a similar relationship, helping each other along, hauling logs and clearing paths.

Bulky Oxen is a beer inspired by food and one dish in particular: The Post's wood-fired pork shoulder with caramelized onion marmalade. It's a dish Selders describes as life changing. Using it as a launching point, the two brewers needed to decide which aspects of the food would best translate into a great beer and focused on caramelization, smoke, and luscious flavors. Bulky Oxen ended up as a deep mahogany, English-style barleywine with a modest ABV. It features rich, lush malt flavors balanced by tropical American hops and citrus peel.

A housemade marmalade made with caramelized, Sucanat sugar-crusted citrus and sweet onion is added during the boil to offer sweet and savory aromas of orange, spice, and smoke. This Strong Ale is the perfect partner for a hearty meal of pork or beef and is equally well suited as a nightcap on a cool evening near a fire.

	Extract	All Grain
Estimated original gravity (OG)		
Estimated SRM		
Estimated IBU's		
Estimated alcohol ABV %		
Suggested fermentation temperature	68°F	68°F

Specific Recipe Information

Start by making some killer onion marmalade. Chop a pound of sweet onions and a half pound of assorted citrus, mix together, and toss with a pound of Sucanat. Smoke or roast all of this on a tray until it's caramelized, soft, and delicious. Puree the whole mixture and hold onto it for a little bit.

Boil your wort. After 5 minutes, add the Columbus hops. Fifty minutes later, stir in the marmalade. Five minutes later, add the Azacca hops and boil for an additional 5 minutes. Turn off the flame, add the Centennial hops, and gently stir to create a nice whirlpool. Cover the kettle and allow the wort to rest for about 20 minutes.

Ferment the beer between 68°F and 72°F. Once the final gravity has been reached, allow the beer to rest at fermentation temperature for 3 to 4 days. Transfer to secondary for 1 to 2 weeks conditioning.

KIT: EXTRACT

Malt Extracts/Additions

13 pounds of Pale Malt Extract

Steeping Grain

1 pound Caramel 80 L (or 77 L)

8 ounces British Chocolate Malt

Use a grain bag. Add to water immediately. Remove steeping grain at 170°F

Hops

0.5 ounces Columbus (19% AA)

0.5 ounces Azacca (14% AA)

1 ounce Centennial (11% AA)

0.75 pounds Sucanat

0.1 pounds Smoked Sweet Onion and Citrus Marmalade

Bittering Hops are boiled for 60 minutes.

Aroma/Flavor Hops are boiled for 5 minutes.

Aroma/Flavor Hops are added at end of the boil.

Marmalade added with 10 minutes left on the boil.

KIT: ALL GRAIN

Hops

Bittering Hops are boiled for 60 minutes.

Bittering/Flavor Hops are boiled for 15 minutes.

Aroma Hops are added at last 1 minute of boil.

1st Dry Hops is added to secondary for 6 to 8 days.

2nd Dry Hops is added to secondary for 3 to 5 days.

Wort Clarifying Treatment

KICK Carageenan (1 Tablet) – Add at last 5 minutes of the boil.

Bottling

4 ounces corn sugar – Boil with 2 cups of water for 5 minutes.

THE RARE BARREL

BERKELEY CALIFORNIA

Beer Name

HOME, SOUR HOME

AMERICAN WILD ALE

The Rare Barrel is an all-sour beer brewery based in Berkeley, California. It houses about 1,000 oak barrels in its cellar, but due to the aging time required for sour beer and the experimental nature of the brewery, it currently can only sell beer out of its own facility.

Its approach to sour beer is uncommon in that The Rare Barrel doesn't have a house culture or a consistent lineup of beers. Instead, the brewery tries to develop many house cultures that will specifically fit certain types of sour beer. Starting with questions like, "What makes the perfect apricot sour beer?" the brewers research the answer with many experimental batches, mixing Saccharomyces, Brettanomyces, Lactobacillus, and Pediococcus in various amounts, times, and temperatures to learn about the full gamut of flavor they will produce. Then they blend to find the best matches for each secondary ingredient. The Rare Barrel rarely sets out to brew an exact type of beer from day one. Instead, it lets the beer's flavor determine its own destiny.

So what makes the perfect apricot sour beer? The founders of The Rare Barrel don't know yet—they view their brewery as a decades-long experiment. Finding new fermentations that produce new, unique flavors and aromas is their passion. In fact, the name of the brewery itself is derived from this very passion. Inspired by the story of the legendary barrel pH1, The Rare Barrel invites their community into their barrel cellar to taste through barrels and find the one barrel that stands above the rest: The Rare Barrel. The beer from that barrel is removed to enjoy and then new wort is added to that same barrel to propagate that special mix of yeast and bacteria that made such an amazing beer.

Making sour beer opens a whole new world of flavors to exploration. Acidity can pair so well with so many things, and Home, Sour Home is no exception. The Rare Barrel set out to create a beer reminiscent of the comfort of home. With that goal in mind, the idea was to make a sour beer that would evoke memories of Peach Cobbler.

A primary fermentation with *Brettanomyces* and *Lactobacillus*, although unusual, creates a terrific base. The Brett aromatics are kept in check, making for a relatively clean aromatic base, while the *Lactobacillus* will sour the beer just enough to simulate the desired acidity.

This base leaves room for the secondary ingredients to shine. Add the peach first and allow it to complete a secondary fermentation before any of the spice additions. Introducing the spice too early will blow off the volatile aromatics of those ingredients.

After a couple of months, the peach re-fermentation should have calmed down, and the beer will be ready for the cinnamon and vanilla. Once another week or so passes, keg or bottle and enjoy. This beer is very special to The Rare Barrel team because of its ability to remind them of home. One last suggestion: Consider brewing this beer to share with loved ones at Thanksgiving. It pairs well with turkey and arguing with the in-laws.

	Extract	All Grain
Estimated original gravity (OG)	1.048	1.048
Estimated SRM	3.5	3.5
Estimated IBU's	1	1
Estimated alcohol ABV %	5.3%	5.3%
Suggested fermentation temperature	70°F	70°F

Specific Recipe Information

Pitch Brett/Lacto in primary at normal ale pitch rates. A starter is recommended.

Once the beer tastes good and fermentation is not visually apparent (4 to 6+ months), add 1 pound per gallon of peaches.

Wait 4 to 12 weeks for the peaches to ferment. Then, add 5 grams per gallon of cinnamon sticks and one tenth of a split in half vanilla bean per gallon.

KIT: EXTRACT

Malt Extracts/Additions

3.5 pounds Extra Light Dry Extract OR

4.5 pounds Pale Liquid Extract

Turn burner off before adding. Boil for 60 minutes.

Steeping Grain

1 pound Malted Wheat

9 ounces Spelt Malt

9 ounces Rolled Oats

6 ounces Vienna Malt (or Sp. Aromatic)

Use a grain bag. Add to water immediately. Remove steeping grain at 170°F.

Hops

A pinch of hops or none at all!

Wort Clarifying Treatment

Whirlfloc (use ½ to 1 Tablet) – Add at last 5 minutes of the boil.

KIT: ALL GRAIN

Grain

6 pounds Pale Malt – 2-Row

1 pound Malted Wheat

9 ounces Spelt Malt

9 ounces Rolled Oats

Recipe based on: 70% Mash Efficiency

Mashing will depend on your preferred fermentation:

Brett Primaries: 145°F

Sacc Primaries: 155°F

Hops

A pinch of hops or none at all!

Wort Clarifying Treatment

Whirlfloc (use ½ to 1 Tablet) – Add at last 5 minutes of the boil.

RELIC BREWING COMPANY

PLAINVILLE CONNECTICUT

Beer Name

ANYSSA
BELGIAN DARK STRONG ALE

Established in February of 2012, Relic Brewing started as a daydream over a glass of homebrew on a sunny deck. Mark Sigman brewed his first batch in 1994 while living in Jackson Hole, Wyoming, and spent years there learning about the burgeoning craft beer industry, enjoying lots of now-classic microbrews, and practicing with recipes.

Years later, he returned to Connecticut and started to take the hobby more seriously. Inspired by beers, ingredients, and ideas he experienced while traveling domestically and abroad on a yearlong break between jobs, he started brewing smaller batches much more frequently. Fascinated by the increasing array of hops, yeasts, and malts available for homebrewers, Sigman spent hours poring over catalogs and Internet sites.

After about a year of governmental red tape, he finally opened his own brewery in a small industrial space in Plainville, Connecticut. The Relic name was inspired by Sigman's extended international trips abroad. While exploring ancient sites across the globe from Peru's Machu Picchu to the pyramids of Egypt and the temples of Angkor in Cambodia,

fermented beverages were always a common theme. And museum after museum had displays of ancient relics used in the production of these beer-like consumables.

Continued and somewhat unexpected demand for Relic beers encouraged Sigman to go full time as a brewer after about six months, and soon thereafter, he began planning various upgrades and expansions. He found his most successful offerings combined full flavored, yet balanced profiles and often an intriguing or unexpected ingredient. Nearly six years and more than 130 beers later, Relic Brewing has become an established and recognized player in the Northeast craft brewing scene.

Although Mark now supervises production of some of the more popular beers at a larger facility, he can still be found brewing creative and experimental batches on the three-barrel Plainville system. And most weekends, he also still enjoys talking beer, recipes, and ingredients with customers and aspiring brewers in the tasting room.

Over the years, Sigman has been most inspired by Belgian beers. In particular, he was drawn to the free-form nature and the use of unusual ingredients as well as various sugars, candi syrups, and honeys. One day, during a mash rest, Sigman began researching unusual honeys to play around with. He had previously used orange blossom, blueberry, wildflower, and raspberry honeys and enjoyed the flavors created by late additions of this ingredient. Unfamiliar with sourwood honey, he read about the tree that only grows in certain areas of the Appalachian Mountains. This prized honey, which can be ordered online from various sites, has wonderful notes of spice and licorice-like anise flavors. He immediately started designing a beer around it.

Sigman went with dark malts and roasty, semi-sweet chocolate flavors in the base recipe since some Stouts have mild licorice notes. Some older recipes even include brewer's licorice. Then, he added American Mt. Rainier hops, which are known to have licorice and anise-like aromas. He also included a touch of ground anise just to help emphasize the flavor. About a week later, the idea of using fennel fronds came to him while eating a salad with fennel in it. Many Relic beers were sparked by ideas and inspiration found at fine restaurants or in the pages of cookbooks. Often, the same flavor combinations that work in cuisine work just as well in beer.

The final beer turned out well and was enthusiastically received in the tasting room and at BeerAdvocate's Extreme Beer Fest in Boston. The key to the recipe is balance—not too sweet, not too roasty, with flavors and aromas of licorice and anise that don't overpower.

	Extract	All Grain
Estimated original gravity (OG)	1.075	1.075
Estimated SRM	32	32
Estimated IBU's	21	21
Estimated alcohol ABV %	8%	8%
Suggested fermentation temperature	68 to 75°F	68 to 75°F

Specific Recipe Information

Add 1 pound Sourwood Honey at end of the boil.

Add ½ teaspoon ground anise at end of the boil.

If bottling: Fronds from 1 to 2 bulbs of organic fennel (depending on amount of fronds) are added at end of the boil.

Cool and Pitch Yeast White Labs Belgian Ale or Equivalent. Ferment at 68 to 75°F until completed, 10 to 14 days.

If kegging: Place fronds from 1 to 2 bulbs of organic fennel in a cheesecloth hop sack and dry hop in keg with beer for maximum aroma.

KIT: EXTRACT

Malt Extracts/Additions

7 pounds Pale DME

Turn burner off before adding. Boil for 60 minutes.

Steeping Grain

1 pound British Chocolate Malt Crushed

1 pound Cara Munich Malt Crushed

0.5pounds Crystal 40 L Crushed

Use a grain bag. Add to water immediately. Remove steeping grain at 170°F.

Hops

60 minutes – Northern Brewer – 0.75 ounces

0 minutes – Mt Rainier – 0.75 ounces

Wort Clarifying Treatment

Irish Moss added at 15 minutes left in the boil.

KIT: ALL GRAIN

Grain

12 pounds British Pale Ale Malt

1 pound British Chocolate Malt Crushed

1 pound Cara Munich Malt Crushed

0.5pounds Crystal 40 L Crushed

Recipe based on:
70% Mash Efficiency

Strike Water Temperature: ~162°F

Mash Temperature: 150°F

Time: 60 minutes.

Sparge Water Temperature: 170°F

Time: 15 minutes.

Hops

60 minutes – Northern Brewer – 0.75ounces

0 minutes – Mt. Rainier – 0.75 ounces

Wort Clarifying Treatment

Irish Moss added at 15 minutes left in the boil.

RIGHT BRAIN BREWERY

TRAVERSE CITY MICHIGAN

Beer Name

THAI PEANUT
BROWN ALE

Right Brain Brewery opened in December of 2007 in Traverse City, Michigan, with a mission to "brew what we want, when we want, because we can." Starting on a seven-barrel brew system, Right Brain Brewery soon became a Traverse City favorite known for brewing big IPAs and culinary-inspired ales using ingredients like beets, honey, cucumbers, or basil.

Inspiration for Right Brain brews often derives from the power of conversation. Founder Russell Springsteen once had dinner with a Mangalitsa pig butcher. At the end of dinner, it was agreed that Right Brain could use the leftover smoked pig heads and bones to brew a Mangalitsa Pig Porter, which won a gold medal at the 2011 Great American Beer Festival in the experimental category. A discussion with a local pie company turned into the Pie Whole series, where Right Brain throws whole baked pies (crust and all) into the fermenter. Calculated, culinary-inspired risks like these have turned out to be some of Right Brain's most sought-after beers and even inspired symbiotic relationships with companies that use Right Brain beer to make their own products.

As distribution demand grew, the need arose for Right Brain to grow as well, and in 2012, it moved into a new 10,000 square foot (929 square meter) production facility and added a fifteen-barrel brewing system. The increased space for brewing production enabled Right Brain to keep up with distribution, while still allowing brewers to make small batches with asparagus, spicy peanut butter, mint, lavender, chipotle peppers, and vanilla, among other ingredients.

Today, everything Right Brain does is guided by the tagline, "Keep Beer Curious." Right Brain is never fully satisfied with what beer is; instead, it's curious about what beer can become with a little creativity and passion. This tagline isn't only a guiding light for brewery employees; it's also a challenge to other breweries to keep pushing the boundaries of beer. It's a celebration that Right Brain is lucky enough, after ten years, to still be brewing "what we want, when we want, because we can."

Have you ever had a tasty Thai dish, and then laid awake all night thinking about how you could make it into a beer? Right Brain Brewery did and then went to work creating a delicious, spicy brown ale called Thai Peanut. Brewing the wort is the easy part of making this beer. Making the spicy peanut butter and adding it to the fermenter is the hard (and fun) part. Right Brain's head chef makes spicy peanut butter in house, but its ingredients (roasted unsalted peanuts, unrefined coconut oil, toasted unsweetened coconut, and red Thai chili peppers) can be purchased at any specialty food store.

It's advisable to make the batch in increments to check the flavor, adding more of certain ingredients as needed. Once the spicy peanut butter is ready, smear it along the inside of the fermentation vessel's walls before adding wort. At the brewery, this process can get pretty messy, so make sure to do it in a space you can clean easily.

The final product is a beer that's a liquid embodiment of a traditional Thai peanut dish and just as spicy, too. Strong aromas of roasted peanuts and chili peppers provide a pleasant nose, while sweet flavors of toffee, caramel, and creamy peanut butter come through with the first sip, followed by a medium level of spicy heat that lingers. Thai Peanut pairs well with pad Thai, Korean barbecue dishes, chicken satay, banh mi sandwiches, or hearty, creamy dishes to cool the heat from this spicy beer.

	Extract	All Grain
Estimated original gravity (OG)	1.068–1.070	1.068–1.070
Estimated SRM	16	16
Estimated IBU's	25	25
Estimated alcohol ABV %	7.7–7.9%	7.7–7.9%
Suggested fermentation temperature	66 to 68°F	66 to 68°F

Specific Recipe Information

Add spicy Thai peanut butter to fermenter before adding wort. Smear on wall of fermenter. How to make Right Brain's spicy Thai peanut butter: Ingredients you will need: 8 to 12 ounces natural organic peanut butter, 1.5 to 2 ounces unrefined coconut oil, 4 to 8 ounces unsweetened, shredded coconut (toast for more flavor), 4.5 to 5 ounces red Thai chili peppers. Clean/sanitize a mixing container and complete the following steps separately:

Process ¾ of the shredded coconut with coconut oil to create a butter/paste. Ratio should be about 4:1. Add the other ¼ of the shredded coconut as is. Melt the rest of the coconut oil and blend into peanut butter. Process the whole chili peppers into a "rough" powder. Please note that seeds will not blend down too much, and this is fine. Blend all ingredients together in a your sanitized container. It's suggested to make peanut butter in increments, taste flavor, and add more of each ingredient if necessary.

KIT: EXTRACT

Malt Extracts/Additions

9 pounds Light Malt Extract

1 pound Dried Malt Extract

4 ounces Maltodextrin

Turn burner off before adding. Boil for 60 minutes.

Steeping Grain

2.62 pounds Vienna

0.95 pounds Crystal 65

0.6 pounds Flaked Oats

0.36 pounds Crystal 45

0.12 pounds Chocolate Malt

Use a grain bag. Add to water immediately. Remove steeping grain at 170°F.

Hops

0.2 ounces Nugget Bittering hops are boiled for 60 minutes.

0.5 ounces Centennial Bittering hops are boiled for 30 minutes.

Wort Clarifying Treatment

Whirlfloc (use ½ to 1 Tablet) – Add at last 5 minutes of the boil.

KIT: ALL GRAIN

Grain

10 pounds 2-Row

2.62 pounds Vienna

0.95 pounds Crystal 65 L

0.6 pounds flaked oats

0.36 pounds Crystal 45 L

0.12 pounds Chocolate Malt

Turn burner off before adding. Boil for 60 minutes.

Hops

0.2 ounces Nugget Bittering hops are boiled for 60 minutes.

0.5 ounces Centennial Bittering hops are boiled for 30 minutes.

Wort Clarifying Treatment

Whirlfloc (use ½ to 1 Tablet) – Add at last 5 minutes of the boil.

RIVERTOWN BREWERY AND BARREL HOUSE
CINCINNATI OHIO

Beer Name

DEATH
RUSSIAN IMPERIAL STOUT

As long as he can remember, Rivertown founder Jason Roeper has had a passion for fermentation. Growing up, he found himself amazed by his uncle, who would spend his weekends brewing and then bring his handcrafted libations to family gatherings. The day Roeper turned twenty-one, he went to his uncle's house and brewed his first batch of beer. He swears it was terrible, but continued to persevere, experiment, and hone his craft.

In search of honest feedback, Roeper began sending his beers to a variety of local and national homebrew competitions and to his surprise, ended up with numerous awards. Despite all his medals, though, he continued to spend time dialing in even the smallest of details on his recipes and while doing this, uncovered a passion for yeasts and bacteria of the wild variety.

In 2007, Roeper decided to submit a beer to the Sam Adams LongShot Competition and became a finalist with Straight Up, his unblended Lambic. Shortly after that experience, he put his vision to paper and began pounding the pavement. Never

accepting "no" for an answer, despite how many times he initially heard it, Roeper finally realized his dream to share his brewing passion with a larger audience in 2009, when Rivertown Brewing Company was born. To this day, the company continues to embrace that determined spirit in everything it does.

Rivertown is part brewery, part lab exBEERiment, part gathering place, and part smokehouse and arcade where research, innovation, quality, and customer exBEERience are the top priorities. The team enjoys perfecting the science behind calculated fermentations as much as it likes to get its funk on with wild and spontaneous fermentations. Working diligently to handcraft a tenacious culture (people, yeast, and bacteria) one beer at a time, Rivertown enjoys the challenge of brewing consistently extraordinary beer that is both noteworthy and timeless. One of its goals is to encourage people to take a sip on the wild side, even if that means starting with something un-tart.

A harmony of heaven and hell, this robust Russian Imperial stout is brewed with a grim dose of Bhut jolokia chilies, also known as ghost pepper. Originally made in 2012 as a part of Rivertown's Four Horsemen of the Apocalypse series, it wasn't long before consumers were begging for the beer version of Death. It's not for the timid. Death offers up a warm, high gravity, roasty, rich, chocolate malt embrace only to displace this mirth with a severe yet balanced kick of heat at the back of the palate. This beer celebrates the conundrum of the soul and may be the only time when through Death, life is found.

For Rivertown, extreme means being fearless and tenacious in everything it does. For those bold enough to brew this beer, Rivertown recommends being bold in experimenting with the Bhut jolokia chilies; try dried, fresh with seeds, or fresh without seeds—just make sure to wear gloves.

	Extract	All Grain
Estimated original gravity (OG)	1.101	1.100
Estimated SRM	40	40.7
Estimated IBU's	30.2	30.2
Estimated alcohol ABV %	11.7%	11.7%
Suggested fermentation temperature	68°F	68°F

Specific Recipe Information

After primary fermentation, rack to secondary and add 2 to 3 whole chopped ghost peppers (in a hop sock) and allow the beer to sit in the secondary for three weeks at 33°F.

KIT: EXTRACT

Malt Extracts/Additions

10.5 pounds Light DME

Turn burner off before adding. Boil for 60 minutes.

Steeping Grain

4 ounces English Dark Crystal Malt

4 ounces Chocolate Malt

1 pound Roasted Barley

Use a grain bag. Add to water immediately. Remove steeping grain at 170°F.

Hops

0.5 ounces Bravo 15.3% AA at 60 minutes.

0.5 ounces Cascade 5.75% AA at 1 minute.

Whirlpool – 1 hop sock of ghost pepper chilies (4 to 6 fresh cut peppers per bag) .

Wort Clarifying Treatment

Whirlfloc (use ½ to 1 Tablet) – Add at last 5 minutes of the boil.

KIT: ALL GRAIN

Grain

18.5 pounds 2-Row Malt

4 ounces Chocolate Malt

4 ounces English Dark Crystal Malt

12 ounces Roasted Barley

Recipe based on:
75% Mash Efficiency

Strike Water Temperature: 162°F

Mash Temperature: 150°F

Time: 90 minutes.

Sparge Water Temperature: 168°F

Time: 40 minutes.

Hops

0.5 ounces Bravo 15.3% AA at 60 minutes.

0.5 ounces Cascade 5.75% AA at 1 minutes.

Wort Clarifying Treatment

Whirlfloc (use ½ to 1 Tablet) – Add at last 5 minutes of the boil.

SHMALTZ BREWING COMPANY

CLIFTON PARK NEW YORK

BITTERSWEET LENNYS R.I.P.A.
RYE DOUBLE IPA

Shmaltz won nine Gold and five Silver Medals in the World Beer Championships in 2012 and was ranked as one of the top 100 brewers in the world by a popular website a year later. A recipient of the Distinguished Business Award by the Brooklyn Chamber of Commerce, Shmaltz was also included in the "Top 50 Fastest Growing Bay Area Companies" by the San Francisco Business Times, and its beers have appeared in numerous distinguished media outlets.

Founder and sole proprietor Jeremy Cowan established the company in San Francisco in 1996 with the first 100 cases of He'brew Beer. Today, Shmaltz is sold across thirty-five states, through forty wholesalers and nearly 4,000 retailers. Change accompanied growth. After seventeen years of being an outspoken cheerleader for contract brewing, Shmaltz broke with its own tradition and opened a production brewery in Clifton Park, New York, ten minutes north of Albany's capital district. Shmaltz's new home features a fifty-barrel brewhouse and 30,000 barrels of annual capacity.

The new brewery packages 12 and 22 ounce (355 and 650 ml) bottles and kegs of the company's diverse core and its seasonal favorites. Their beer also comes in 12 and 16 ounce cans. Several new releases and collaborations were introduced in 2016, and Shmaltz continues its acclaimed exploration of barrel aging with a current inventory of more than 300 bourbon, rye whiskey, and tequila barrels.

The 1,700 square foot (158 square meter) tasting room is a place where visitors can sample a variety of fresh Shmaltz beers, tour the facility, and learn about the beer-making process. In Clifton Park, they can also witness Shmaltz's signature borscht belt humor. Depending on the time of year, visitors to the tasting room might find a beer menorah display that includes empty bottles from the gift pack or a T-shirt with the slogan "Don't Pass Out, Pass Over."

Bittersweet Lenny's Rye IPA is an American double IPA made with an extreme amount of rye malt. Shmaltz brews its RIPA with 20 percent malted and flaked rye along with select crystal, caramel, and aromatic malts to provide a rich, smooth, and spicy drinking experience. But no self-respecting IPA is complete without hops. Shmaltz uses a cross section of American hops from high alpha varieties like Warrior all the way to low aromatic hops like Amarillo to provide a bold bitterness and a crisp piney, spicy nose complemented by a whirlpool addition of ground caraway that lends the perfect rye bread aroma.

Bittersweet Lenny's Rye IPA pours a brilliant chestnut brown with a slightly tan head that dissipates to gorgeous lacing that will chase the beer down to the bottom of your glass. It will also leave you feeling enriched the same way the famed comedian Lenny Bruce, this beer's namesake, so often left his audiences.

	Extract	All Grain
Estimated original gravity (OG)	1.094–1.098	1.094–1.098
Estimated SRM	16-18	16-18
Estimated IBU's	80-90	80-90
Estimated alcohol ABV %	9.5-10%	9.5-10%
Suggested fermentation temperature	65°F	65°F

Specific Recipe Information

Primary Fermentation, approximately 10 days.

0.75 ounces each of Amarillo, Centennial, Simcoe, and Crystal dry hop at secondary fermentation.

KIT: EXTRACT

Malt Extracts/Additions

7.5 pounds Light Malt Extract

Turn burner off before adding. Boil for 60 minutes.

Steeping Grain

2 pounds Rye Malt

10 ounces Flaked Rye

5 ounces Kiln Amber

5 ounces Wheat Malt

4 ounces Crystal 65 L

4 ounces CaraMunich 60 L

2 ounces Crystal Rye

Use a grain bag. Add to water immediately. Remove steeping grain at 170°F.

Hops

1.5 ounces Warrior is boiled for 90 minutes.

0.5 ounces each: Cascade, Simcoe, and Warrior are boiled for 20 minutes.

0.5 ounces each: Cascade, Crystal, and Chinook are boiled for 10 minutes.

1.25 ounces Centennial+ 0.5 ounce each: Amarillo, Cascade, and Simcoe are added at end of the boil.

Wort Clarifying Treatment

Whirlfloc (use ½ to 1 Tablet) - Add at last 5 minutes of the boil.

KIT: ALL GRAIN

Grain

9 pounds 2-Row

2 pounds Rye Malt

10 ounces Flaked Rye

5 ounces Kiln Amber

5 ounces Wheat Malt

4 ounces Crystal 65 L

4 ounces CaraMunich 60 L

2 ounces Crystal Rye

Turn burner off before adding. Boil for 60 minutes.

Hops

1.5 ounces Warrior is boiled for 90 minutes.

0.5 ounces each: Cascade, Simcoe, and Warrior are boiled for 20 minutes.

0.5 ounces each: Cascade, Crystal, and Chinook are boiled for 10 minutes.

1.25 ounces Centennial+ 0.5 ounce each: Amarillo, Cascade, and Simcoe are added at end of the boil.

Wort Clarifying Treatment

Whirlfloc (use ½ to 1 Tablet) - Add at last 5 minutes of the boil.

SHORT'S BREWING COMPANY

BELLAIRE MICHIGAN

BLOODY BEER

FRUIT/ VEGETABLE BEER

In a way, Short's Brewing Company began as a DIY project when founder Joe Short was still a student at Western Michigan University. After learning to homebrew at age nineteen to avoid finding someone old enough to buy beer for him, Short developed a love and passion for brewing that soon took priority over a college degree. So he took a reprieve from school and began a brief stint in the Michigan brewing scene. Not long thereafter, Short and friends restored an old hardware store and Short's Brewing Company was born in the tiny village of Bellaire, Michigan, in the spring of 2004. The goal was simple: Short's would become a community brewery that would distribute draft locally, serve up simple deli style food, pour high quality beer, and bring live music to Bellaire.

At the pub, a broad range of styles such as Local's Light, Soft Parade fruit ale, and Huma Lupa Licious IPA were brewed on a seven-barrel system in the basement and graced the faucets upstairs. From the early days it was important to cover all styles to serve a demographic of people new to craft brewing's diversity of flavor. In 2007 Short's began crafting more experimental and specialty beers with the Imperial Beer Series. This project would shape the future of Short's brewing style, leading to a more explorative and nontraditional approach to making beer.

Beer enthusiasts finding their way to Northern Michigan generated excitement, and the brewery evolved rapidly in an effort to keep pace with production demand as well as the pub's increasing popularity. With more experimental and specialty beers drawing attention to the brand, Short's opened a production facility in Elk Rapids in 2009 to release bottles throughout the state of Michigan for the first time. Meanwhile, the original pub and brewery quickly outgrew its original design. The release of the Greatest Hits Menu inspired by the band Ween, was followed by the first pub expansion in 2010, which included kitchen upgrades and increased seating capacity. Multiple subsequent expansions in both Bellaire and Elk Rapids have accommodated more guests and beer alike.

After exclusively distributing beer in Michigan for over a decade, Short's decided to enter new markets in 2016. It continues to champion creatively fearless beers and the exploration of innovative and experimental brewing. With hundreds of beers already in the portfolio, Joe and the Short's team look to the future with an unlimited supply of creative ideas they plan to employ in beers in the years ahead.

Bloody Beer is a lightly hopped golden beer made with Roma tomato, black peppercorn, celery seed, fresh dill, and horseradish. Joe Short chose California Common yeast because to him, it produces "good beer." It's technically a lager fermented at ale temperatures, which provides a great base for this special concoction. Short, who has always enjoyed a splash of beer in his Sunday afternoon Bloody Mary recipe, thought he'd add some Bloody Mary to his beer. He had heard of successful homebrewed tomato ales and had seen people add tomato juice to their beers, so making this beer seemed completely doable and delicious. One of the strengths of this Bloody Beer recipe is how well it works with so many different ingredients, but this is only one version and serves as a great baseline for further experimentation.

Tomatoes are rich in calcium, potassium, and vitamins A and C. They're also a good source of lycopene, which is an anti-oxidant and a powerful carotenoid. Covering pain relief, indigestion, colic, fever, stomach aches, and in some cases inhibiting food pathogens, spices like pepper, dill, celery seed, and horseradish have long been valued for their health properties. It's no wonder then that the Bloody Mary has been an infamous hangover cure with all of the benefits it possesses from the tomato juice and spices. Fernand Petiot is said to have invented the Bloody Mary cocktail in Paris in the 1920s. He mixed equal portions of vodka and tomato juice together and with the eventual evolution of a little Worcestershire sauce, cayenne pepper, and lemon, the classic cocktail was born. This beer will go great with almost anything, especially a big piece of garlic toast, fried eggs, hot sauce, and locally smoked bacon.

	Extract	All Grain
Estimated original gravity (OG)	14.8 plato	14.8 plato
Estimated SRM	13.39	13.39
Estimated IBU's	40	40
Estimated alcohol ABV %	7%	7%
Suggested fermentation temperature	65°F	65°F

Specific Recipe Information

Wash and de-stem 6 pounds of fresh ripe roma tomatoes. Sterilize the roma tomatoes by boiling in water for 10 minutes. Puree 6 pounds of hot sterilized roma tomatoes. Add the hot sterilized roma tomato puree into the primary fermenter before adding chilled wort. Do not pitch California Common yeast until the chilled wort has cooled down the hot puree and you have achieved an overall fermenter temperature of 65 to 70F. Once fermentation is complete, add 0.5 ounces ground peppercorns, 0.5 ounces celery seed, 0.25 ounces fresh dill, and 0.25 ounces prepared horseradish into the primary. Let spices steep for 7 days before crash cooling the fermenter.

KIT: EXTRACT

Malt Extracts/Additions

5 pounds Light Malt Extract

Turn burner off before adding. Boil for 60 minutes.

Steeping Grain

2.5 pounds Ashburn Mild

2.5 pounds Bonlander Munich

Use a grain bag. Add to water immediately. Remove steeping grain at 170°F.

Hops:

0.5 ounces Perle (7.6 AA%) at 60 minutes.

0.5 ounces Perle at 30 minutes.

0.5 ounces Perle at whirlpool

Wort Clarifying Treatment

Whirlfloc (use ½ to 1 Tablet) – Add at last 5 minutes of the boil.

KIT: ALL GRAIN

Grain

6 pounds 2-Row

2.5 pounds Ashburn Mild

2.5 pounds Bonlander Munich

Turn burner off before adding. Boil for 60 minutes.

Recipe based on: 70% Mash Efficiency

Hops:

0.5 ounces Perle (7.6 AA%) at 60 minutes

0.5 ounces Perle at 30 minutes

0.5 ounces Perle at whirlpool

Wort Clarifying Treatment

Whirlfloc (use ½ to 1 Tablet) – Add at last 5 minutes of the boil.

SOLEMN OATH BREWERY
NAPERVILLE
ILLINOIS

SCAREBALL
IMPERIAL PILSNER

Solemn Oath Brewery was founded in 2012 in the Chicago suburb of Naperville, Illinois, with a fifteen-barrel brewhouse and a focus on American and Belgian styles along with the occasional "extreme" seasonal selection. Until it introduced rotating 22 ounce (650 ml) bombers into the Chicagoland market in early 2013, Solemn Oath was draft-only. In 2016, the brewery completed an expansion, which doubled the size of the brewhouse and introduced 12-ounce (355 ml) cans.

Today, Solemn Oath produces two year-round canned brands, Snaggletooth Bandana IPA and Funsponge Belgo-American Blonde, in addition to numerous seasonal beers in draft and bomber format. Currently, Solemn Oath beers are available throughout Illinois and select areas of Wisconsin. Besides a three serving limit per person per day, the Naperville taproom operates by a simple set of rules: no cash, no tips, just beer.

The concept behind Scareball is to impart some of the more dynamic attributes of an American double IPA into the existing flavor profile of a German Pilsner, those attributes being hop-malt balance, an elevated ABV, and a bright, fresh hop aroma. The malt profile in this recipe is simple and straightforward: bready, with slightly honeyed sweetness and a smooth, round mouthfeel from high-quality Pilsner malt. This base layer is accentuated by the generous use of Noble-type hops in both flavor and aroma. Assertive without being overly bitter, Solemn Oath uses a blend of Mt. Hood, Czech Saaz, and a whisper of New Zealand Motueka for a bold, spicy, grassy hop profile with subtle notes of lime citrus. Resist the urge to add any American hop beginning with the letter C—the goal isn't to make a double IPL.

Of course, the most important aspect of brewing this style is fermenting it with characterful lager yeast. Solemn Oath works with the Wyeast 2007 Pilsen Lager strain due to its ability to produce a clean, neutral flavor profile with subdued ester formation, light sulfur character, and a dry finish. For the best outcome, ferment cold, be patient, and make sure your yeast is in good condition, as the higher ABV should exist subtly beneath the other flavors. The result is a hop-forward lager, bright enough to satisfy a hophead, yet smooth and drinkable with a clean, dry finish.

	Extract	All Grain
Estimated original gravity (OG)	1.076	1.076
Estimated SRM	3.7–4.3	3.7–4.3
Estimated IBU's	70–80	70–80
Estimated alcohol ABV %	8.5%	8.5%
Suggested fermentation temperature	50°F	50°F

Specific Recipe Information

Mash at 149°F.

Dry hop schedule:
2/3 lb./bbl Czech Saaz
1/3 lb./bbl Motueka

KIT: EXTRACT

Malt Extracts/Additions

13.5 pounds Pilsner Malt Extract

12 ounces Maltodextrin

Turn burner off before adding. Boil for 60 minutes.

Steeping Grain

None

Hops

Nugget – 50 BU at 0 minutes

Mt. Hood – 10 BU at 60 minutes

Motueka – 5 BU at 60 minutes

Mt. Hood – 5 BU at WP

Motueka – 5 BU at WP

Wort Clarifying Treatment

Whirlfloc (use ½ to 1 Tablet) – Add at last 5 minutes of the boil.

KIT: ALL GRAIN

Grain

Weyermann Barke Pils – 90%

Briess Carapils – 10%

Recipe based on:
70% Mash Efficiency

Strike Water Temperature: 160°F

Mash Temperature: 149°F

Time: 30 minutes

Sparge Water Temperature: 168°F

Hops

Nugget – 50 BU @ 0 minutes

Mt. Hood – 10 BU @ 60 minutes

Motueka – 5 BU @ 60 minutes

Mt. Hood – 5 BU @ WP

Motueka – 5 BU @ WP

Wort Clarifying Treatment

Whirlfloc (use ½ to 1 Tablet) – Add at last 5 minutes of the boil.

STRANGEWAYS BREWING

RICHMOND VIRGINIA

MUST BE NICE, WHITE WINE SOUR

AMERICAN WILD ALE

Neil Burton, the founder of Strangeways Brewing in Richmond, Virginia, has always had a penchant for exploring the unknown, especially when it comes to beer. As a result, he has found himself in some of the more peculiar corners of the world tasting as many different beers as possible and returning with a profound passion for, and an acute knowledge of, implausibly good beer.

Combining this fixation on great beer with his appetite for the unfamiliar, Burton embedded himself in Virginia's burgeoning craft brewing culture. Realizing he didn't want to merely be a spectator, though, he began tirelessly working toward what would eventually become Strangeways Brewing. At first, he intended to create a new beer brand by utilizing someone else's brewing facility in an alternating proprietorship. However, he quickly discovered that the law wouldn't allow for such an arrangement. So, working with Virginia legislators, he set to change the law. But by the time House Bill 359 passed, Virginia's mushrooming craft brewing industry had experienced such historic growth that breweries no longer had the capacity to make their space available to others.

It could have been kismet, or random luck, that Burton met longtime brewer Mike Hiller at the governor's signing of House Bill 359. Either way, the two turned out to be nothing short of a natural pairing. Once they combined Burton's industry knowledge and entrepreneurship with Hiller's extensive brewing experience, all the pieces fell into place. Their mutual desire to use the finest ingredients, pursue the imperfect, entertain their curiosity, and add an element of anomaly to the brewing world is what fuels the strange in Strangeways Brewing.

Founded in 2013, Strangeways has produced over 300 different beers on its twenty-barrel brewhouse in just four years. Its one-of-a-kind taproom and production facility houses multiple indoor and outdoor tasting spaces, always has at least thirty-six unique Strangeways beers on tap, and is open to the public daily for tastings, tours, and special events. One of the tasting room spaces houses an exquisitely peculiar bar laden with hundreds of curious oddities and breweriana pieces. Another allows visitors to view the brewhouse alongside a backdrop of over 200 spirit and wine barrels, where a wide variety of beers are silently aging for future enjoyment.

Must Be Nice, White Wine Sour is a dry, tart beer that exhibits a lovely white grape character, supported by effervescent carbonation and a refreshing acidity. To achieve this, Strangeways Brewing employs both *Lactobacillus* aging in barrels and its own version of kettle souring, which involves a modified fermenter to sour the wort. Homebrewers should use whichever process works best for them.

After kettle souring, Strangeways brought the wort to a boil and added hops and white wine grape juice. To lay down a nice, dry finish, since it usually hits a very low final gravity, the brewery fermented first with a Saison yeast, perfect for lower pH worts. After the primary fermentation, the beer was transferred to neutral oak barrels to age for several weeks with another addition of white wine grape juice and a dose of Champagne yeast. The Champagne yeast will go to work on the sugars remaining after primary fermentation and those in the added white wine grape juice, but leave behind a distinctive, pleasant grape flavor. If you don't have access to an appropriately sized oak barrel, try using French oak spirals for an added depth of oak character. Use a slightly higher dose of priming sugar when bottle conditioning because this beer is much more brilliant with a sparkling, prickly carbonation.

Must Be Nice, White Wine Sour would also make a terrific base beer for branching out beyond the flavors imparted by the white wine grape juice. Consider experimenting with spring and summer fruits like cherries or peaches. Perhaps some ginger and honey in secondary fermentation would be a nice touch, too. The possibilities are endless.

	Extract	All Grain
Estimated original gravity (OG)	1.040	1.040
Estimated SRM	Light, man. Real light.	Light, man. Real light.
Estimated IBU's	13	13
Estimated alcohol ABV %	4.8%	4.8%
Suggested fermentation temperature	72°F and free rise	72°F and free rise

Specific Recipe Information

Lactobacillus souring can be done one of two ways:

1) Kettle souring in which Lactobacillus is added to kettle or carboy, and the wort kept at 110°F to 115°F for 24 to 48 hours targeting a pH between 3.2 and 3.4;

2) Adding Lactobacillus to post fermentation aging for several weeks. Add 64 ounces of white wine grape juice to the boil for 5 minutes.

Ferment with Saison yeast and allow temperature to free rise – artificially dropping temperature can result in stuck fermentation. Add another 64 ounces of white wine grape juice to secondary fermentation with champagne yeast and age for 1 month.

For authenticity, add French oak spirals to secondary fermentation with white wine grape juice and champagne yeast

KIT: EXTRACT

Malt Extracts/Additions

3.5 pounds Extra Light Malt Extract

Turn burner off before adding. Boil for 60 minutes.

Steeping Grain

1 pound Honey Malt

0.5 pounds Golden Naked Oats (regular oats if GNO not available)

Use a grain bag. Add to water immediately. Remove steeping grain at 170°F.

Hops

0.25 ounces Saaz (3% AA) for 60 minutes

0.2 ounces Nelson Sauvin (12% AA) for 30 minutes

0.15 ounces Nelson Sauvin (12% AA) for 15 minutes

1 ounce each: Nelson Sauvin, Pacific Gem, El Dorado at whirlpool (0 minutes).

Yeast

Belgian Saison Yeast

KIT: ALL GRAIN

Grain

5.5 pounds Pilsner Malt

1 pound Honey Malt

0.5 pound Golden Naked Oats (Rolled Oats if GNO not available)

Turn burner off before adding. Boil for 60 minutes.

Recipe based on:
70% Mash Efficiency

Strike Water Temperature: 144°F

Mash Temperature: 156°F

Time: 30 minutes

Sparge Water Temperature: 168°F

Time: 20 minutes

Hops

0.25 ounces Saaz at 60 minutes

0.20 ounces Nelson Sauvin at 30 minutes

0.15 ounces Nelson Sauvin at 15 minutes

64 ounces white wine grape juice at 5 minutes

1 ounce each: Nelson Sauvin, Pacific Gem, El Dorado at whirlpool (0 minutes).

Yeast

Belgian Saison Yeast

TREE HOUSE BREWING COMPANY

GREENFIELD MASSACHUSETTS

Beer Name

WINTER IS COMING

IMPERIAL STOUT

The story of Tree House began in a small red barn in the warm spring of 2011. Nate Lanier had been brewing fanatically at home for a while when his good friend Damien Goudreau purchased a house with a detached barn. The barn gave Lanier the space to really flesh out his ideas, and it wasn't long before the two were planning the path for their little brewery.

Tree House opened its doors in the spring of 2012 with a ten-gallon (3.8 L) brewing system. The crowds were huge since day one, and the team has been scrambling to get ahead of demand ever since. In six years, Tree House went from a ten-gallon (3.8 L) fully manual system, to a five-barrel fully manual system, to a thirty-barrel fully manual system, and most recently, a sixty-barrel fully automated German-designed brewhouse. The brewery also moved three times, and Tree House is currently building its second Greenfield brewery in two years. When that project is complete, it will have a state-of-the art brewery that will help the company produce core beers like Julius, Green, and Haze consistently and in sufficient quantity, while its existing thirty-barrel brewery becomes an incubator for more innovative, boundary pushing projects.

Tree House Brewing's Number 1 goal is to make the best beer in the world and to serve it in the friendliest and most comfortable environment possible. It's an obsession shared by the whole team, and it's what drives them to do what they do.

For *Project Extreme Brewing*, Lanier wanted to design a beer that was interesting, rich with complexity, and above all, bold. The beer builds on a simple Imperial stout recipe with the addition of flaked oats, a healthy amount of molasses, and an assortment of crystal malts. A longer boil also adds to the depth of character, creating a beer that is mysterious, intensely flavorful, and well suited for long-term aging. Better still, Winter Is Coming also serves as a stage for further experimentation. Once you've made the original, try personalizing it by changing the recipe with your own tastes in mind.

	Extract
Estimated original gravity (OG)	1.123
Estimated SRM	43.7
Estimated IBU's	59.79
Estimated alcohol ABV %	10.93%
Suggested fermentation temperature	

KIT: EXTRACT

Specific Recipe Information

Ferment with English Ale Yeast (WLP002) at 68°F. Target water profile is Ca2: 100, Mg2: 10, Na: 0, Cl: 0, SO4: 0,HCO3: 0.

Malt Extracts/Additions

21 pounds Pale Malt Extract

1 pound molasses

Steeping Grain

1.5 pound Flaked Oats

1 pound Crisp Pale Chocolate Malt

1 pound Roasted Barley

8 ounces Caramel 120 L

8 ounces Caramel 60 L

4 ounces Special B Malt

Use a grain bag. Add to water immediately. Remove steeping grain at 170°F.

Hops

2 ounces Magnum

Wort Clarifying Treatment

KICK Carageenan (1 Tablet) – Add at last 5 minutes of the boil.

Priming Sugar added at Bottling

4 ounces corn sugar – Boil with 2 cups of water for 5 minutes.

TROPHY BREWING COMPANY
RALEIGH
NORTH CAROLINA

Beer Name

THE KING
BELGIAN-STYLE DUBBEL

Trophy Brewing began as a daydream. In 2009, Chris Powers and Woody Lockwood had just opened The Busy Bee Cafe, a craft beer-focused restaurant in downtown Raleigh, North Carolina. The two immediately began a barrel program in which they worked closely with local and regional breweries to make special beers that were dreamt up and designed for aging in specific barrels and casks with exciting ingredients. It wasn't long before the two friends' passion for bringing fun, exciting, and creative beer ideas to the glass manifested itself in the desire to open a brewpub.

As daydreams go, one fun suggestion led to the next, and a true vision for a brewpub began to emerge—one that embraced the nostalgic, quirky childhood desire for a shelf of plastic trophies. Soon, ideas began to flow, like tap handles made from inexpensive trophy parts, and beer names like Lord Stanley and Trophy Wife. Even subtle artistic allusions to the sign of a well-known downtown trophy store worked their way into the brewery's logo. Les Stewart, a friend and passionate homebrewer, shared the partners' vision for American craft brewing and where to take it. In 2012, he joined the team as brewmaster. Then, the three worked for the better part of a year to design and squeeze a three-barrel brew system and pizza kitchen into a tiny space on West Morgan Street.

History then began to write itself. Featuring outside-the-box beers with creative and mostly local ingredients and a pizza kitchen that embraced a similar philosophy, the brewpub became successful beyond expectations. The following years came with such on-site demand that in spite of packing additional fermenters into the small brewery, Trophy was unable to even keep all of its draft lines flowing with its own beer. Once the team had tasted the magic of brewing, they wanted to not only make enough beer for themselves, they also wanted to be able to provide beer to the greater Raleigh community. And so began the work on the next incarnation of Trophy Brewing—it was time to build a second facility, this one with a twenty-barrel brewhouse and space for barrel aging.

The second facility opened in December of 2015 near the North Carolina Farmers Market and only minutes from the original location. At the new location, Trophy now has the ability to simultaneously produce a larger volume of favorite established brands as well as age its beers in a variety of barrels. As an added bonus, Trophy also now has the opportunity to develop new and experimental recipes at the original location.

The King, a reference to Elvis Presley's favorite midday meal, is best described as a Peanut Butter Banana Sandwich Belgian-style Dubbel. Trophy first developed this beer for BeerAdvocate's 2013 Extreme Beer Festival in Boston. The idea was born in a rash of midnight texts between Powers, Lockwood, and Stewart about a beer that might best fit the theme of the festival. The beer has since evolved to feature local North Carolina products: boiled peanuts, peanut butter, and honey.

The malt bill for the base beer is most similar to a Belgian-style Dubbel, while a Bavarian Weizen yeast known for producing big banana aromas is employed to round out the concept. The key to the beer, however, is the way that the boiled peanuts and peanut butter is integrated. In the years since, The King has become a favorite beer for Trophy with a special place in the hearts of the Trophy partners and its followers. Although only brewed once or twice a year, The King has the ability to draw a crowd when its release is announced.

	Extract
Estimated original gravity (OG)	1.067
Estimated SRM	
Estimated IBU's	11.5
Estimated alcohol ABV %	6.5
Suggested fermentation temperature	

KIT: EXTRACT

Specific Recipe Information

Use a peanut butter with as few ingredients as possible, ideally just peanuts, salt, and honey. We use Macky's Ferry Peanut Butter produced in small batches in eastern North Carolina. Adding the peanut butter to the boil: First spoon the entire 0.5 pounds of peanut butter into a muslin bag. Place the bag into a smaller pot. At 30 minutes into the boil, remove some boiling wort from the kettle and add it to the smaller pot along with the honey. With the back of a large spoon, massage the peanut butter through the sides of bag allowing it to dissolve into the wort. Once the liquid in the smaller pot has become cloudy brown, pour the liquid back into the kettle, keeping the muslin bag in the smaller pot. Repeat the process a few times until all that is left in the bag is a substance harder and darker than what you started with. This remainder represents the most insoluble aspects of the peanut butter and should be discarded.

Malt Extracts/Additions

10 pounds Pilsen Malt

1.5 pounds Aromatic Malt

1 pound Victory Malt

0.5 pounds Munich Malt

4 ounces Honey at 30 minutes

0.5 pounds Peanut Butter at 30 minutes

0.5 pounds "Green" Peanuts for Boiling : Secondary fermentation

Use a grain bag. Add to water immediately. Remove steeping grain at 170°F.

Recipe based on: 70% Mash Efficiency

Strike Water Temperature: 165°F

Mash Temperature: 152°F

Time: 60 minutes

Sparge Water Temperature: 175°F

Hops

0.75 ounces Hallertaur at 60 minutes

Yeast

WLP351 or Wyeast 3068

Wort Clarifying Treatment

Whirlfloc (use ½ to 1 Tablet).

MARZ COMMUNITY BREWING
CHICAGO, ILLINOIS

ADAORA NIGERIAN LAGER
FRUIT/VEGETABLE BEER

To understand the Marz Community Brewing's origin story, you must start with the place we call home. Bridgeport, Chicago, the "community of the future," is the true definition of diversity, collaboration, and struggle, all of which went into starting our brewery in 2012.

The Marz collective is comprised of homebrewers, professional brewers, and artists that found each other while drinking beers at Maria's Packaged Goods & Community Bar. Our love of our neighborhood and good beer inspired us to create a new experience for natives and visitors to Bridgeport.

Making beer five barrels at a time allows us to expand on our creativity, play with our emotions, and ultimately get to the place we always feel most comfortable: weird. Although the plan was to stay small in a space on the south side of Chicago, our story has taken a turn. With popular beers like Jungle Boogie (an American Pale Wheat Ale with rooibos tea) and Ruby's Tears (a Gose with coriander and hibiscus) we are riding the wave of hard work, grit, and good fortune all the way to our new facility, which is set to open in late 2017. Once it does, we'll be able to more than quadruple our production.

So as we say on the South Side: We will see you'se around campus. Look for our beer nationwide as of... now.

Lager beer is widely consumed in Nigeria. This lager-style beer incorporates traditional spices and ingredients common to the country and significant to Nigerian culture in a way that creates a flavor profile different from any lager you have ever tasted. But it is not extreme just for the sake of being extreme. Each ingredient holds significance to Nigeria's Igbo people and the country as a whole.

Breweries in Nigeria typically utilize sorghum in their mash because it's a widely grown grain. Limits are set on the importation of barley to encourage the use of locally grown sorghum. Bitter kola is extremely important to Nigerian culture, specifically for the Igbo tribe in southeastern Nigeria where it is eaten at most gatherings of importance: weddings, funerals, naming ceremonies, the meeting of elders, etc. In the recipe, kola powder is added to the boil. Alligator pepper is often presented in the same bowl with bitter kola at important events. It is similar to grains of paradise with a fruity, black pepperlike quality.

Mangos are one of Nigeria's major fruit exports. In this spiced up lager, mango puree brings a noticeable tropical note. Since palm products are used widely in Nigerian cuisine, palm sugar is added at flame out. Nigerians often use the red oil from palm trees in cooking soups and stews. It's interesting to note that in Nigeria, once palm sap is collected it immediately begins fermenting due to the natural yeast and bacteria in its tropical climate. This produces palm wine within hours, which is consumed nationwide.

	Extract	All Grain
Estimated original gravity (OG)	1.050-1.055	
Estimated SRM	4-8	
Estimated IBU's	30-35	
Estimated alcohol ABV %	5.5	
Suggested fermentation temperature	58 to 68°F	

Specific Recipe Information

Grains of Paradise may be substituted for the Alligator Pepper.

Alligator Pepper/Grains of Paradise should be moderately crushed before use.

The Kola Nut species used was cola acuminata.

Carbonate to 2.6 volumes of CO_2.

KIT: EXTRACT

Malt Extracts/Additions

3.3 pounds Sorghum LME

3 pounds Pilsen Light DME

0.5 pounds Palm Sugar

Fruit/spice additions

0.5 ounces Bitter Kola Nut Powder: Added to wort during the last 10 minutes.

7 grams Alligator Pepper: Flame out addition

5 grams Alligator Pepper: Secondary fermentation

7 pounds Mangoes, Organic: Secondary fermentation

Hops

2 ounces El Dorado: Boiled for 15 minutes

0.5 ounces El Dorado: Added to wort at flame out

Wort Clarifying Treatment

Whirlfloc (use ½ to 1 Tablet) – Add at last 5 minutes of the boil.

KIT: ALL GRAIN

Grain

5.5 pounds Continental Pilsner

3.3 pounds Sorghum LME

0.5 pound Palm Sugar

Recipe based on:
70% mash efficiency

Strike water temperature: 60°F

Mash Temperature: 148°F

Time: 60 minutes

Sparge Water Temperature: 175°F

Fruit/spice additions

0.5 ounces Bitter Kola Nut Powder: Added to wort during the last 10 minutes

7 grams Alligator Pepper: Flame out addition

5 grams Alligator Pepper: Secondary fermentation

7 pounds Mangoes, Organic: Secondary fermentation

Hops

2 ounces El Dorado: Boiled for 15 minutes

0.5 ounces El Dorado: Added to wort at flame out

Wort Clarifying Treatment

Whirlfloc (use ½ to 1 Tablet) – Add at last 5 minutes of the boil.

CHAPTER 3 EXTREME BREWING AROUND THE WORLD

I do believe the extreme brewing movement began in America and has gone on to influence and enhance the craft brewing cultures in other countries around the world, but I wanted to be sure this perspective wasn't that of a sloppy, arrogant, mis-informed American. So, I asked a few renowned beer experts from other countries to answer two straightforward questions to provide a global context to our movement and to add a few more sage voices to the robust chorus of strong voices contained within this book.

Q&A WITH JÖRGEN HASSELQVIST

OLIVER TWIST BAR & RESTAURANT
STOCKHOLM, SWEDEN

1. HOW DO YOU THINK THE CRAFT BREWING REVOLUTION IN THE U.S. HAS INFLUENCED THE BREWING SCENE IN SCANDINAVIA?

Oh, it really started everything I would say. Not brewing, of course, but to add your imagination and curiosity. Europe and Scandinavia have long histories and traditions within brewing, but when that first smell of cascade hops came around, it blew everyone away, especially me! After that, I just had to find out more about what was going on in the U.S. and certainly try and get some beers!

Now, Swedes, and Scandinavians in general, are quite reserved when it comes to new trends and when it comes to beer, too. But, in this case, it was a huge wake-up call for the brewing community—not for the big boys, they've started to copy things in the past two to three years, but for all those people with a dream to do and brew something different. It all started with you guys in the States for sure: to maybe start a business within brewing and actually brew what you want to brew, realizing that there was people out there desperate for new flavors and styles!

2. HOW DO YOU PERSONALLY DEFINE EXTREME BREWING, AND WHAT IS YOUR FAVORITE LOCAL EXAMPLE OF AN EXTREME BEER?

I guess extreme brewing to me pretty much means using everything but malt, hops, and "standard" yeast; or adding all sorts of things into the brew, exploring what can happen, and if it ends up good and drinkable, or not—I sure have had both! I have had some amazing extreme beers, but of course, some bad ones too.

A local favorite would be Stockholm Brewing Co.'s Hallon Sour (Raspberry Sour). I really like sours; also Brekeriet and Brewski in the south of Sweden are doing some amazing beers.

FROM JEAN-FRANCOIS GRAVEL

BRASSERIE DIEU DU DIEL
MONTREAL, CANADA

In the early days of the craft beer revolution, around the mid-1980s, most breweries in Canada were making English- and German-style beer. In Quebec, however, probably due to our linguistic connection, we had access to a lot of imported beer from Belgium: Rodenbach, Chimay, Orval, and Dupont, to name a few. These brewers seemed very open-minded in comparison to English and German brewers. So, using Belgian beer as an example, several brewers in Quebec started to brew strong beer with spices and different cereals and among the most adventurous, wild yeast and bacteria. Around the mid-1990s, we started noticing that American brewers had also begun making more interesting beers as well.

In the mid 1990s, nobody in Canada could have imagined a beer dry hopped at 2 pounds (900 g) per barrel with a now iconic hop like Citra. Now, due to the influence of the American craft beer revolution on the Canadian beer scene, we came to think differently about hops in terms of the variety and also the way in which we use them. Previously, we thought of hops in terms of traditional bittering or aroma varieties, but new hop varieties coming out of the U.S. that were selected for flavor started becoming available. We also started to manipulate how we used hops in the brewing process, specifically the timing and quantity, in order to bring out the characteristics we were looking for.

Extreme brewing could be seen simply as making beer that is very high in alcohol with a massive quantity of hops; however, there's a lot more to it than that. It's also playing with different aspects of the brewing process and using nontraditional ingredients to create or accentuate a different flavor.

Sometimes, it means pushing the limits to the point where you wonder if it's still even a beer. In this new world of craft beer culture that's not tied to tradition, we have the freedom to play with the characteristics of any beer. You go to a restaurant or to the market, you taste a fruit, a spice, and an herb, and boom, you've got a new idea for a beer! Brewing extreme beer means that even if it is good, it might not please everyone, but it can also appeal to people looking for an alternative to fizzy, flavorless yellow lager.

Over the years, we've brewed a lot of extreme beers, but Rosée d'Hibiscus is a prime example of what I mean when I talk about extreme brewing being more complex than just a 15% ABV, 200 IBU beer. First brewed in 2006 for a beer festival, this beer was designed to catch people's attention and appeal to both new and experienced craft beer drinkers. It's a pink, hibiscus-infused wheat beer that's a hybrid between West African bissap juice and a Belgian wit. At 5.9 percent, it smells like roses but is tart like cranberry juice. It's just a little bitter and not at all sweet, and it pairs easily with seafood, poultry, or dessert. I never could have imagined that this beer would become one of the main products at our packaging brewery.

Q&A WITH LORENZO DABOVE

1. HOW DO YOU THINK THE CRAFT BREWING REVOLUTION IN THE U.S. HAS INFLUENCED THE BREWING SCENE IN ITALY?

Without a doubt, our rapid and exciting craft beer revolution was influenced decisively by the American one. On a smaller scale, even our early pioneers, as well as the Americans, reacted to the overwhelming power of the tasteless industrial mass market lagers, first proposing beers inspired by classic styles of Belgium, Germany, and the United Kingdom. Soon, our artisans, encouraged by me in Italy and Charlie Papazian from the United States and during his early trips with overseas brewers, began to create, as it was in the States, indigenous styles with local ingredients. It is very important that our brewers, despite using American or New Zeland hops, do original beers from the famous creativity and imagination that is recognizably Italian.

Our fortunate brewers benefit from the extraordinary biodiversity of products, such as different varieties of grains, herbs, vegetables, and fruits that allow them to create bold and innovative beers. These are two of the key factors of the success of our beers in the world.

The revolution is expanding all over the planet. Italy is now a leader in Europe in terms of fostering a creative national brewing community.

All this could not have happened without the decisive influence of the American Brewing Revolution, for which we are all eternally grateful.

2. HOW DO YOU PERSONALLY DEFINE EXTREME BREWING, AND WHAT IS YOUR FAVORITE LOCAL EXAMPLE OF AN EXTREME BEER?

I would define an extreme beer as one that is characterized by great freedom of expression of a maverick brewer. I would compare an extreme beer to an acrobat who does his exercise at 100 meters (328 feet) high looking for a challenging but rewarding balance.

A brewer can make extreme beers using traditional ingredients but in a different way, using unusual techniques and in huge quantities unthinkable only a few years ago. But, in most cases, to get to the extreme beers, the brewer uses strictly local ingredients, little known elsewhere and especially almost never used before.

Extreme beers are very exciting and challenging for both producers and consumers and a source of inspiration for the growing number of homebrewers.

I really like to be a judge in the category of experimental beers to find aromas and flavors not discovered before. Extreme beers are the opposite of the bland industrial beers; they are the pride of producers who are also researchers and experimenters.

We have many examples of extreme beers in Italy and in the new field of wild and sour beers, both in the bold use of local ingredients. Having to name just one significant example, I would choose one of those brewers that produces extreme beers not for trend but for vocation. Riccardo Franzosi, brewer of Birrificio Montegioco, lower Piedmont, uses local grapes for his I.G.A. (Italian Grape Ale), the first brand new Italian beer style ready to be included in the BJCP guidelines.

Furthermore, he uses the extraordinary fruits of his beloved land in all possible ways to achieve beers all focused on compliance with the time of maturation and aging: The Quarta Runa with Volpedo peaches, the Garbagnina with Garbagna cherries, the Magiuster with wild strawberry from Tortona, and the Moronina with mulberries—All extreme in their conception but all devoted to the pleasure without exceeding in acidity so much that I call "gently sour."

Finally, we have in Italy extreme beers with basil leaves, tobacco and eucalyptus, spelt, enkir, and kamut grains; then chestnuts, locust bean, chicory, rosemary, mountain pine, gentian, thistle, prickly pear, bigarade, rose petals; and who knows what else will be born in the future!

AFTERWORD

BY SAM CALAGIONE

I took my first baby steps on this journey just after college when I tried my first few craft beers, read *The Joy of Homebrewing* and Michael Jackson's first book, and began homebrewing with culinary ingredients in early 1993. Within another year, I had written my business plan for Dogfish Head around the ideal of creating the first commercial brewery committed to brewing the majority of our beers outside the Reinheitsgebot, incorporating culinary ingredients in our creative process. A year later, in 1995, we opened for business. That same year, one of my favorite bands of all time, Guided by Voices, released their album *Alien Lanes*. I listened to that album (on cassette on a boombox—yup, I'm old) many times on many brew-days that first year Dogfish was open, as I pumped out batches of beers like Raison D'Etre (raisins and beet sugars) and Chicory Stout (roasted coffee and chicory). I loved the music

on the album but I also remember whispering the name of the album and the band to myself as I brewed or hunkered down and waddled the fermenters back to the cooling rack. Guided by voices ... alien lanes ... guided by voices ....

I have written elsewhere about the beautiful symmetry and overlapping trajectory of the three American artistic movements most dear to me that grew up together and into the mainstream simultaneously: hip-hop, indie rock, and craft brewing. All three started as grassroots movements from tiny but growing networks of artists, influencers, and enthusiasts. The lines between these roles were and still are enticingly blurry. An indie rock critic would become the bassist in an indie rock band, a hip-hop producer would become a star MC, a fearless homebrewer would become a fearless craft brewery owner.

When I opened my brewery, and this album came out, I repeated the album and band name as a mantra largely because those words describe the journey I was on and that moment on the journey. In my business and in my creative process, I was not guided by the mainstream. I was not guided by or interested in following the first generation of craft breweries who opened doors for breweries like Dogfish Head with their well-made, super-fresh, super-flavorful but also true-to-historic-style pale ales and Hefeweizens. I was "guided by voices" in my head—By the voices of patron saints of creative brewing like Charlie Papazian and Michael Jackson and patron saints of creative self-reliance like Walt Whitman and Ralph Waldo Emerson.

These were "alien lanes" back in the mid-nineties. There were a few breweries making occasional beers with culinary ingredients (shouts to Anchor Christmas Ale) but we were the first to make it our main focus, and there were no easy routes to market for 11 percent ABV smoked maple syrup beers or 90 IBU Imperial IPAs in the late 1990s. The lanes that were available to get your beer on to retail shelves back then were mostly defined with hard and fast guardrails: distributors and retail stores had slots for light lager and pale ale and amber and wheat beer. Slots for fruit-infused IPAs did not exist. Thankfully, just in the nick of time, a few "alien lanes" begin to open up. BeerAdvocate become the online destination for curious and adventurous beer drinkers, the Great American Beer Festival began diversifying their beer judging categories to include experimental beers, and The Extreme Brewing Festival came to life in a small round room in downtown Boston. This community of artists, influencers, and enthusiasts found each other, bolstered one another, and helped this movement grow.

I wrote the first Extreme Brewing in 2006 with the help of a handful of creative American craft brewers like Vinnie (Russian River), Tomme (Lost Abbey), Adam (Avery) and Rob (Allagash). To do "research" for that book, I invited these four brewers to join me on a trip to Belgium, a country that has some inspiring brewing traditions. We had a wonderful time rubbing and bending elbows with Belgian brewers and beer enthusiasts. Generally, they were complimentary and open-minded as they tried the exotic beers from our breweries that we brought to share with them. But sometimes, they would shake their heads or laugh politely at our quixotic brewing and ingredient decisions. They had some beautiful creative brewing traditions, but they were still adamant about following the traditions of their brewing culture more than they were interested in reinventing it for themselves as we were as American brewers. We did meet a few young Belgian brewers who were more open-minded to our approach, and we have stayed close and mutually supportive with them since that trip. When it was time for me to put the call out for recipes for that book, in addition to the four mentioned above, there were a handful of other super-creative American craft brewers following their own muse and creating truly unique beers who graciously agreed to include their recipes in that book.

Today's vibrant and diverse beer landscape is the greatest testament to how far the Extreme Brewing movement has come in the decade since the five of us took that trip to Belgium, and that change can most easily be described by how easy it was for Jason, Todd, and I to find such a wide range of inspired, inventive, individualist brewers to contribute their recipes and philosophies of creative brewing for Project Extreme Brewing. Essentially, the curating process went something like this: We walked around a joyful room full of adventurous beer brewers and adventurous beer lovers and asked a bunch of the brewers we admire and know if they want to participate in this book and project. Every single one we asked said "Hell yes. Count me in." That's what makes this community so awesome: This openness; This altruism; and this willingness to share. To share our knowledge and brewing secrets with homebrewers is a concept that would seem strategically unorthodox in most other industries, but ours is a community first and an industry second.

It's inspiring for me to read about the way the American Extreme Brewing movement has influenced other brewers in other countries and how they have applied that adventurous spirit to inform their journeys of evolving their own provincial creative beer scenes. And this inspiration flows between each creative brewer in each country, and the more we share with each other, the stronger and louder we collectively are. We are guided by voices that have been amplified to eleven since the early days of the extreme brewing movement. The alien lanes are a lot more plentiful and accessible than they were in the early days. As a homebrewer, we are glad you have put your turn signal on by buying this book and are hopefully ready to become an extreme brewer in your own right.

The album Alien Lanes, like Dogfish Head, has just turned twenty-one, the legal drinking age, as I type this afterword in the fall of 2016. I want to leave you with a quote from an article on the music website celebrating the twenty-first birthday of this album.

"The trebly bombast and pronounced discursiveness of Alien Lanes was read as typical indie caginess in 1995, but 21 years later it's this tension between (lead singer Robert) Pollard's bigtime rock classism and self-defeated sonic fuckery that's aged best. In retrospect, Alien Lanes can be viewed as a nexus point in rock history, representing the end of an era when the record business believed that a band like this could make a million dollars, the beginning of our current era in which rock is essentially folk music, where it is kept alive not out of financial imperative, but because rock can act as a safe space for people who have consciously decided to ignore financial imperatives and exist outside of the mainstream culture." Written by Steven Hyden on Pitchfork.com.

Sam

AFTERWORD

BY TODD AND
JASON ALSTRÖM

Extreme beer isn't just about brewing something different. It's about thinking differently. It's about approaching the entire beer experience differently, from raw ingredients to stimulating the drinker's pleasure center and inspiring their palates to never settle for the norm again.

We discuss this philosophy with brewers during every Extreme Beer Fest®, as we taste their brews and listen to the passionate stories behind each creation. Unfortunately, these lubricated exchanges are often lost after the moment, so it's truly awesome to finally capture the thinking behind some of these creative beers and share them with you.

We've been tasting and critiquing commercial beers for over two decades now, but in our experience, the only way to really get to know a beer at its core is when you've designed, brewed, nurtured, and packaged it yourself. This concept is lost on most critics and self-appointed experts who've never brewed a batch of beer in their lives. And this level of appreciation is something that only brewers (home or professional) get and one that only deepens when it's shared with others. Hopefully, your own appreciation for particular beers and extreme brewing in general will grow as you use this book.

Like we said at the beginning of the book, it's been a while since we last homebrewed, but working with Sam on *Project Extreme Brewing* has inspired us to brew again. We plan on starting by attempting to re-create some of the recipes collected here, and we're hoping that you're as stoked as we are to try them—and maybe even find a favorite.

For those of you who have yet to experiment with extreme brewing or, like us, haven't homebrewed in ages, *Project Extreme Brewing* aims to inspire you to brew (and think) outside of the box. And when you do, we'd love to hear your feedback. Drop us an email (mail@beeradvocate.com) or visit our homebrewing forum on BeerAdvocate.com and share your extreme brewing stories. Just don't forget to share your beer first.

Respect Beer®.

Jason & Todd Alström
Founders, BeerAdvocate

ACKNOWLEDGMENTS

FROM SAM:

I hope it's obvious why I steadfastly use the royal WE in the context of authorship of this book. Technically, the legal contract for this book is signed by Jason, Todd, and myself, but we all agree we have proudly acted more as curators, cat-herders, and cantankerous catalysts for cajoling contributors to join us in documenting this journey. I thank the Alströms firstly; our (patient) editor Jonathan and everyone at Quarry books; Chris Graham for his technical brewing leadership, test brewing, and additional writing and editing on this project; Dogfish Head brewer Bill Marchi; and all of the creative brewers whose own voices and recipes are included here within. We made this book come to life together. And now, with the help of a few million or so yeast cells, you, dear reader, intrepid-homebrewer, will add your voice to OUR story as you brew your versions of these recipes and maybe take your own baby steps off the page and onto your own creative brewing path to tweak and morph these recipes and bring them to life through the nurturing of your own barbaric yawp.

FROM TODD AND JASON:

Our names are on the cover, however, like our website, magazine, and beer fests, this book is an idea that required us to rally and work with other passionate people in order to make it successful.

Thanks to our friend, Sam, for inviting us to partner with him on this project; all of the brewers for accepting our invite, for pushing the boundaries of brewing, and for sharing their stories in extreme brewing; Ben Keene and Rebecca Kirkman from BeerAdvocate for lending us their awesome editorial and brewer wrangling skills; Jonathan and the rest of the team at Quarry Books for their patience; and you, the reader, the homebrewer, and the beer geek who's willing to join us as we raise a fist at the norm and push the boundaries of brewing.

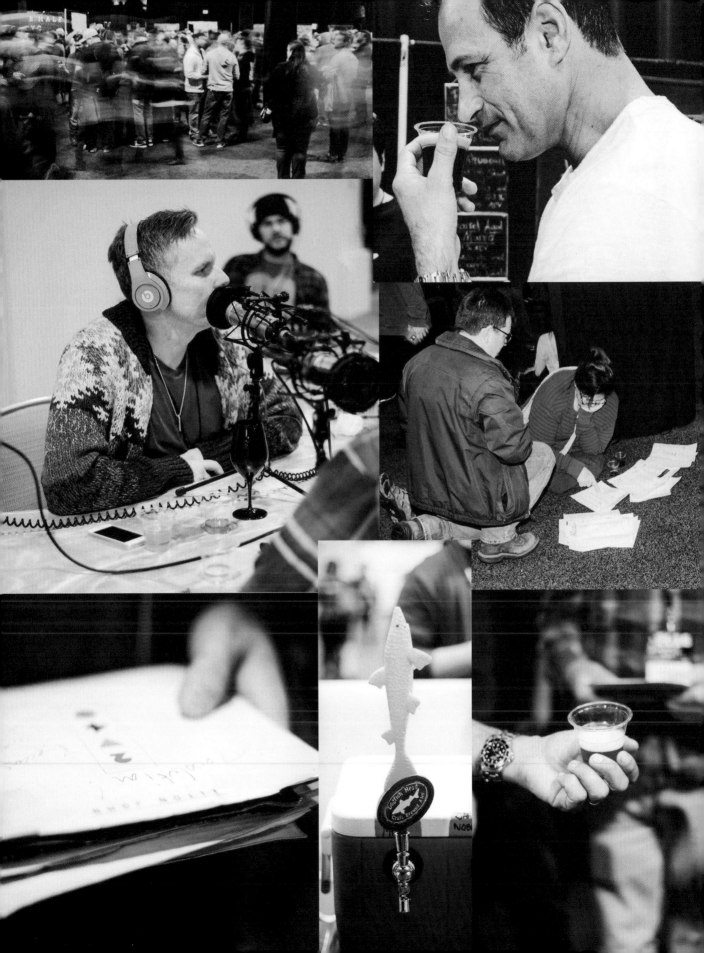

ABOUT THE AUTHORS

SAM CALAGIONE

is the founder and owner of Dogfish Head Craft Brewery, one of the nation's fastest-growing independent breweries. His innovative style has earned him a James Beard Award and a reputation as one of the country's most adventurous brewers.

JASON AND TODD ALSTRÖM

are the founders and publishers of *BeerAdvocate*, widely considered the go-to resource for beer in print and online. They're also the minds behind Extreme Beer Fest®, the ultimate throwdown of brewing creativity.

INDEX